Living Your Strengths

A Positive Psychology Approach

by

David E. Mullen, Ph.D.

AuthorHouse™
1663 Liberty Drive, Suite 200
Bloomington, IN 47403
www.authorhouse.com
Phone: 1-800-839-8640

AuthorHouse™ UK Ltd.
500 Avebury Boulevard
Central Milton Keynes, MK9 2BE
www.authorhouse.co.uk
Phone: 08001974150

First published by AuthorHouse 10/16/2007

ISBN: 978-1-4343-1685-1 (e)
ISBN: 978-1-4343-1684-4 (sc)

Library of Congress Control Number: 2007903884

Printed in the United States of America
Bloomington, Indiana

This book is printed on acid-free paper.

GRATITUDES

A book is never the effort of one person. I am indebted to many others who provided the examples and inspiration to write a book about living an authentic, engaged and compassionate life. They live their strengths. I believe this is what happiness is all about. The influence of the following people impacts this work and I am grateful to them. Hopefully, as they read this book, they will see their footprints. As one of my favorite Beatles' songs remind us, " I can get by with a little help from my friends." Whatever limitations this book has are mine alone. Case examples from my clinical practice have been disguised to protect confidentiality.

I want to acknowledge these individuals. My friend and colleague, Dr. Richard James, first gave me the idea of turning what were initially talks into a book, and presenting some of the ideas to his psychiatric study group. Thanks, Rick. Dr. Tom West, my friend, mentor, colleague and exemplar of the compassionate life, first introduced me to humanistic psychology when I was pursuing a master's degree in psychology. Tom, your influence on me has run deep. Thanks, also, to the Eckerd College students in the first positive psychology class I taught. They offered me important feedback and challenged me to present the material in a user-friendly way. Norm Middleton, office mate, colleague and kindred spirit, we have been through a lot in over twenty years. Your encouragement and experience as published author was a much- needed sounding board for my initiation into the joys and travails of writing a book.

Dr. Shane Lopez, professor of psychology at the University of Kansas and a leader in the world of positive psychology, provided encouragement and support to write this book. Despite carrying a heavy academic load and becoming a father for the first time during the writing of this book, you provided a helpful critique on an earlier draft of this work. Thanks, Shane! I wish you had been on my doctoral dissertation committee! Thanks, too, to a friend and colleague, Dr. Sayers Brenner, who read the manuscript and offered counsel and encouragement during those times when the well went dry and the writing did not come. I am especially grateful, too, for the feedback from my hair stylist, Clara Ahlquist and dear friends and retired teachers, Keith and Jan Robinson. They are laypersons and not academics or clinicians. Your insistence on making the writing intelligible and free from psychological jargon was important. I wrote this book with you in mind.

Finally, I want to acknowledge the love and support of my wife, Judy, my soul mate, dearest friend and love of my life: this book is for you.

FOREWARD

I always have been intrigued by the subtle differences between people that make big differences in the quality of their lives. As a kid I wondered how I did well in school while others struggled. I didn't think I was any smarter than them; I know I didn't work harder. In college, for a lack of a better explanation, I duped myself into thinking, "Maybe I am blessed with analytical intelligence that others did not have and that is why I succeed." Years of research and a handful of publications later, I found that cognitive abilities express less than a third of the variance associated with any meaningful life outcomes. Back to the drawing board!

Over the last ten years, I have become personally and professionally open to the hypothesis that living your strengths lead to a better life. More specifically, I have come to believe that putting myself in situations that allow me to use my strengths creates more opportunities to experience joy, love, engagement, meaning, professional success, and happiness in my life. Daily, I test this assumption. For example, I attempt to practice gratitude (one of my signature strengths) and this "habit" has opened me up to a wealth of joy. Saying "thank you" helps me savor and stretch out the kindnesses bestowed on me and it leaves me with a desire to do more good in the world. (And, I am often reinforced for this practice by friends and loved ones who say that they "cherish" such expressions of thanks.

In this book, David Mullen, a positive psychologist dedicated to make people's lives better, gives you all the tools you need to realize how living your strengths can change your life. Discover your strengths, turn them inside out, and use them like you would your favorite coffee cup or your most comfortable shoes, Why not, these strengths are yours and you should be intentional in how you use them.

Shane J. Lopez

University of Kansas

Lawrence, Kansas

INTRODUCTION

This book is about an exciting movement of psychology, positive psychology, and some of its discoveries about what makes for the good life. While the question, what is the good life is one that has been thought about, wrestled with and reflected on for centuries, what is fresh about this approach is that empirical, well controlled studies verify what philosophers and the great spiritual traditions have been telling us about the role and importance of gratitude, optimism, kindness for well being and happiness.

This book is written for a general audience. While of necessity there are references to some of the leading spokespeople in the field, I have kept them to a minimum. My purpose is not to write a scholarly work, as there are many fine books available (see bibliography) but rather to help the reader connect some of the major themes of positive psychology to their life. For this reason, there are exercises at the end of each chapter. Hopefully, the exercises will help the reader make the connection.

At the outset, let me tell you a little about myself. I wear a number of hats: psychologist, minister, licensed marriage and family therapist. I consider myself blessed to do things I deeply love: to help people live fuller and richer lives through counseling and teach students entering the fields of psychology and counseling. Since a book is often partly autobiographical, I would like to share a few things with you, my reader, about who I am and why a book on positive psychology.

My interest and fascination with human strengths and potential probably first began in high school. Like many teens, I did not know what I wanted to do with my life, let alone choose a career. It was through the encouragement of my mother and others who believed in me and saw potential that I certainly was not aware of, that gave me incentive to keep searching. My father, who worked very hard to keep our family of five afloat, himself as a teen at 16 had to support his family when his father died, was a powerful example of the resilient and resourceful spirit. These themes of encouragement and resourcefulness have been very important personal strengths throughout my life.

As a senior in high school, through a series of experiences, I felt God was calling me to use my gifts in the ministry. After college, I went to seminary and married. My first pastorate was in a small tobacco town in North Carolina during the early sixties. This was a time of much social unrest—especially in the South. The first sit-ins began in Greensboro, North Carolina and then spread throughout the South. Despite the Supreme Court Decision Brown vs. Brown in 1954 there were still segregated schools, rest rooms, fountains, etc. Like many young pastors I became involved in the civil rights struggle and actively opposed our nation's involvement in Vietnam. I thought I could get my church to lead the way in civil rights in our community. In retrospect, I see how naïve I was about how change takes place in the church.

The impact of this on me was disillusionment about the church as a force for social change and social justice. The disillusionment continued to grow even after a second and third pastorate. Questions about staying in the professional ministry continued to plague me. I finally decided to leave the professional ministry. Since then, I have had peace within my soul. I do respect those ministers who can maintain their integrity and be faithful to their calling and lead a church that comforts the afflicted and afflicts the comfortable, but the pastoral ministry was not my cup of tea.

In retrospect, I found that the most satisfying aspects of the professional ministry was counseling and being a witness to and companion with others in some of the seasons of their lives--transitions, suffering, illness, and dying. It is not surprising, then, that I decided to become a psychologist. After all, psychologists and other mental health types have become the "secular priests" of our time. Instead of the confessional, there is the fifty-minute hour; instead of forgiveness of sins, there is acceptance and unconditional positive regard. Needless to say, there are many former priests, rabbis and ministers who are now licensed mental health professionals.

As a graduate student in the '70's, I was drawn to humanistic psychology. The writings of Carl Rogers, Abraham Maslow and Rollo May resonated with me. The emphasis on exploring the farther reaches of human nature (Maslow), the fully functioning person (Rogers) and anxiety as a necessary and creative force in human growth (May) and man's quest for meaning (Frankl) was very exciting. These writings built a link between psychology and spirituality. Over the years, the boundary between psychology and spirituality continues to be a source of deep professional and personal interest to me.

What is positive psychology? Is it an updated version of popular thinking? Some new age movement? Some syrupy, feel-good fad? Is it a "put on a happy face" on the hurts life sends us?

It is none of these. To understand positive psychology, one needs a brief refresher course on psychology. Before World War II psychology had three missions: curing mental illness, making the lives of all people more productive and fulfilling, and nurturing gifted persons. With the advent of WWII, most psychologists turned their attention to treating mental illness. After the war, with recognition by the government and reimbursement for treatments, many psychologists treated those scarred by war and other calamities. The advantages were that advances were made in treating discernible mental disorders. Large grants were given to academics to study various forms of pathology. What was missing was emphasis on the other two distinct missions of psychology. Social psychologist David Meyers did a word search in a major psychology database. He found over 4,000 entries for depression, less than 60 for joy. Psychology became a science largely about healing. It concentrated on repairing damage within a disease model of human functioning.

The emphasis was on treating human deficits and limitations. A whole organized body of knowledge about mental illness developed from this effort, culminating in the first "Bible" of the mental health professions, the *Diagnostic And Statistical Manual Of Mental Disorders* in 1952. The emphasis was on treating pathology. Like psychiatry, psychology focused on what is wrong with human nature, creating as some critics have proposed, a culture of victims. This culture of victimhood was immortalized in the words of comic Flip Wilson's character, Geraldine, "The Devil made me do it!"

In contrast to this emphasis on the deficit and disease model of human nature, positive psychology investigates what is right about human nature. It looks at strengths and virtues, the ingredients of the pleasurable, meaningful and good life. It does not deny or gloss over humanity's dark side. It simply is arguing for a balance. The best of human nature as well as the worst is worthy of psychological investigation. It looks at the factors that allow individuals, communities and societies to flourish.

Perhaps some of you may be wondering if positive psychology is a reworking of humanistic psychology. Popular in the '60's and '70's, humanistic psychology was touted as the Third Force in Psychology, the other two being psychoanalysis and behaviorism. Its chief architects, Abraham Maslow and Carl Rogers, were interested in exploring human potentials—the farther reaches of human nature as Maslow put it. They argued that psychology had become a "rat psychology", reducing the person to s stimulus-response organism that could be manipulated and controlled. For them what was missing in psychology was equal attention to such areas as creativity, beauty, freedom, will, and spirituality. Unfortunately, humanistic psychology was not welcomed into mainstream psychology because it did not attract much of a cumulative empirical base.

It did, however, spawn many therapeutic self-help movements. One need only browse the self-help shelves at the local bookstore to see how psychological self-help has become a huge business. Writes Mihaly Czikzentimihaly, one of the founders of positive psychology: (2002) "...the 'psychology' section contains at least 10 shelves on crystal healing, aromatherapy and reading the inner child for every shelf of a book that tries to uphold some scholarly standard (p.7)"

Positive psychology is not a pop psychology movement. It is an emphasis on what is right about human functioning. Treatment is not just fixing what is broken; it is nurturing what is best. Writes Martin Seligman (2002): "Psychology is not just a branch of medicine concerned with illness or health; it is much larger. It is about work, education, insight, love, growth and play. And in this quest for what is best, positive psychology does not rely on wishful thinking, faith, self-deception, fads, or hand warming; it tries to adapt what is best in the scientific method to the unique problems that human behavior presents to those who wish to understand it in all its complexity (p. 7)."

Two personal stories told by the leading spokespeople of positive psychology explain how they came to the conclusion that such a movement was needed. Martin E. P. Seligman relates the first, a few months after he was elected president of the American Psychological Association. Seligman, professor of psychology at the University of Pennsylvania, was pulling weeds with his five-year-old daughter, Nikki. Seligman, a very goal and task-oriented person, was concerned with getting the weeding done. His daughter on the other hand was thoroughly enjoying herself, throwing weeds into the air, singing and dancing. Seligman yelled at her. She went away and then came back. Seligman continues the story: "Daddy I want to talk to you." "Yes, Nikki?" "Daddy, do you remember before my fifth birthday?

From the time I was three to the time I was five, I was a whiner. I whined every day. When I turned five, I decided not to whine anymore. That was the hardest thing I've ever done. And if I can stop whining, you can stop being such a grouch."

For Seligman, this was an "aha-experience." He learned something about himself, Nikki, childrearing and his profession. He realized that raising children is much more than fixing what is wrong with them. "It's about identifying and nurturing their strongest qualities; what they are and are best at, and helping them find niches in which they can best live out these strengths." (p. 7).

Mihaly Csikzentmihaly, professor of psychology at the Claremont Graduate University, relates the other story. He realized the need for a positive psychology in Europe during World War II. As a child in war-torn Europe he as fascinated by the individuals who kept their integrity and purpose while others were crumbling. These were not necessarily the most educated or most respected or most skilled. What source of strength did these people draw on? What vision did they see? He was intrigued about the vision of meaning that compelled them to be their best. He read history and religion and found their answers unsatisfying. He then was drawn to psychology but also found its answers unsatisfying because psychology at that time was concerned primarily with quantification and measurement. What was lacking was a vision of what the human being could be. His dissatisfaction led him to do studies on creativity, how being fully engaged in whatever one is doing leads to a fuller and richer life. He studied people from all walks of life, including artists, rock climbers, athletes, writers, and workers on assembly lines. We will look at his significant discoveries in chapter 3. One of his ideas is that when we are engaged in a task that is challenging but not overwhelming or stretches our abilities but is doable, we experience a state of flow—a subjective sense of contentment.

I have chosen to limit the scope of this book. Decisions had to be made regarding what topics to include and which to omit. The guiding motivation was to present some of positive psychology's leading ideas in ways that can be useful to the reader. The topics to be discussed are happiness, flow and signature strengths, optimism, hope, gratitude, resilience, forgiveness, and spirituality. As a way to connect the ideas to the reader's life, suggested exercises are at the end of each chapter. In my view, the most effective learning takes place when we can link what we know to what we do; that is, when we can translate ideas into action. I invite the reader to adopt an attitude of curiosity toward these exercises. I hope you will try them.

CONTENTS

GRATITUDES...v

FOREWARD ix

INTRODUCTION xiii

Chapter One: HAPPINESS.....................................1

Chapter Two: FLOW AND SIGNATURE

STRENGTHS 22

Chapter Three: OPTIMISM.....................................42

Chapter Four: HOPE...57

Chapter Five: GRATITUDE 72

Chapter Six: FORGIVENESS 91

Chapter Seven: SPIRITUALITY 110

Chapter Eight: RESILIENCE 128

Chapter Nine: KINDNESS 149

Chapter Ten: INTEGRITY.....................................170

Chapter Eleven: CAN POSITIVE PSYCHOLOGY

SHOW THE WAY?...194

END NOTES 200

FURTHER READING...208

1
HAPPINESS

Happiness depends, as Nature shows, less on
exterior things than most suppose.

William Cowper, 1782

One of the tenets of the Declaration of Independence
is "life, liberty, and the pursuit of happiness." For many,
this is the American dream: the dogged and unrelenting
search for happiness. Over time the meaning and
sources of happiness have changed, depending upon
the cultural emphasis. For our forefathers, happiness
was establishing a new country, the freedom to pursue
ones goals and practice one's religion. With the advent

of the Industrial Revolution in the 1800's, happiness often was linked with material consumption. Such linking had the blessings of the Protestant ethic, which believed that being economically successful was a sign of blessing from God, being one of God's elect. The advent of capitalism and the Protestant work ethic as Max Webber described it became intertwined. Happiness became equated with economic prosperity

Despite the fact that we Americans are affluent by world standards, able to drive nice cars, live in large, clean houses, and have access to entertainment media, we are subjected to high levels of stress. As a result, many of us carry with us a pervasive feeling of discontent. We go after the next highest goal in our lives, only to find that achieving it does not bring us the feelings of true happiness that we long for. Most of us live better than royalty in the past, but these high standards of living have not brought us a sense of true contentment. A recent survey of people in nations around the globe revealed that the highest levels of personal happiness were found in Nigeria, followed by Mexico. Prosperous, industrialized nations like the United States, Canada and most of Western Europe scored at much lower levels.

This chapter is concerned with three questions. What is happiness? Who is happy? How can happiness be increased? We will be drawing upon the discoveries of positive psychology to answer these questions.

HAPPINESS DEFINED

The central objective of positive psychology is the scientific pursuit of optimal human functioning. Martin Seligman, who wrote a best selling book on the subject (2002), describes happiness as both positive emotions (i.e., serenity or joy) and positive states such as those involving flow or gratitude and living your strengths. He classifies positive emotions into three categories: those associated with the past, present and future. Positive emotions such as satisfaction,

3

contentment, fulfillment, pride and serenity are related to the past. Attitudes associated with the future include hope, optimism, confidence, faith, and trust. Positive emotions associated with the present are momentary pleasures and more enduring gratifications. Momentary pleasures are such delights as sex, fragrant perfumes and delicious flavors. More enduring gratifications are more complex and include feelings such as bliss, ecstasy and comfort. Such gratifications we experience when we are using our signature strengths (see chapter 3) and are in flow. To experience happiness, then, we must include both the momentary pleasures and the more enduring gratifications.

Like many ancient philosophies and spiritual traditions, an important idea of positive psychology is that seeking happiness for its own sake does not lead to long-term happiness. To understand this, we must note the difference between pleasurable and enjoyable positive experiences. We experience pleasure when we satisfy basic needs such as hunger, sex and bodily comfort. These feelings are short-lived. We experience enjoyable feelings on the other hand when we stretch ourselves, when we break through some of our self-imposed limits ----completing a mini-marathon, learning to play a musical instrument, public speaking. Enjoyment in these terms leads to personal growth and long-term happiness.

WHO IS HAPPY?

There have been many studies investigating how happy most people are. Diener and Myers conducted one of the most comprehensive. They collected data from 916 surveys of happiness, life satisfaction and well-being involving over a million people in 45 nations around the world. The major conclusion of the study was that the average person is moderately happy (7.5 on a 10 point scale where 0 = very unhappy, 10 = extremely happy). Other studies have found that neither age, gender nor race is important for predicting happiness. While in poor countries such as China, India, being economically well off predicts increased happiness   In affluent countries where most can afford the necessities of life, affluence does not matter that significantly. In the United States, Canada, and Europe, the correlation between income and personal happiness, is "surprisingly weak (indeed, virtually negligible)" (p. 241)

Self-reports of happiness tend to be fairly reliable. Abraham Lincoln said, "Most people are as happy as they make up their minds to be." There is validation to these reports as those closest to the individuals reporting agree. Many people have found that if you feel happy, you are happy. Research has also found that those who report happiness score higher on other indicators of wellbeing. Compared with those who are depressed, happy people are less self-focused, less hostile and abusive, and less vulnerable to disease. They are also more loving, forgiving, trusting, energetic, creative, sociable and helpful.

While there is some evidence for a genetic set point that influences experiencing happiness, it is not fixed. A new model of happiness that addresses this issue is Dr. Sonja Lyubomirsky's model developed with Ken Sheldon and David Schlcade. They suggest that our current level of happiness is determined by three factors: (1) our genetically determined set range of happiness, (2) our unique life circumstance, and (3) our intentional thoughts and behaviors. Let's look at this model more closely. According to Sonja, our happiness set point is largely genetically determined. We come into the world with a genetically determined predisposition toward a certain level of happiness. Some people are effortlessly happy. There are others who find it hard to express joy and experience happiness. Fortunately, those at this low level do not have to stay there.

The second factor that determines happiness is our life circumstances. This accounts for only 10% of current happiness. Life circumstances are both demographic (age, sex, marital status) and contextual (having a baby, getting fired or promoted). The same context could add or detract from happiness. For example, I am a married woman, have a lovely home and have been trying to get pregnant. I find that I am pregnant and I am joyful and happy. I am a fifteen-year-old girl who got pregnant by the guy down the street who sold me drugs. Now I have to quit school to take care of my baby. Different context—different levels of happiness.

Psychologists have demonstrated that people tend to adapt very quickly to positive and negative life events. In one study, people are surveyed one year later after a major life event such as sustaining injuries in an automobile crash or winning the lottery. They tend to go back to the levels of happiness before these major life events. The bottom line is that increases or decreases in happiness due to life events tend to be short-lived. Often we will read in the paper about lottery winners who were worse off (less happy) after their windfall.

What, then, can produce an enduring change in our happiness? This leads to the third factor in the model, intentional activities. This accounts for 40% of our current happiness. Intentional activities refer to those thoughts and behaviors that require effort. Such activities may only be apparent to us or to others. We deliberately engage in activities that make us happy. Our practices may be mental. For example, we decide that we are going to regularly adopt a positive or optimistic attitude. We will not allow other people to determine our mood. Perhaps we decide to change our behavior. We decide to be kind to others. Ian McLauren, the Scottish preacher, wrote, "Be kind to one another for most of us are fighting hard battles." Or having read how regular exercise can lift our moods and give us a natural high, we work out at a local gym. My friend Norm loves golf. He has been known to paint his golf balls red so he can see them when he's playing in a dusting of snow. If you were to ask Norm to rate his happiness level while he's shooting a great game, his answer would blow the top off the chart. Perhaps we volunteer for a group that benefits the homeless or the poor. You might want to reflect here. When are you the happiest? What do you love to do? What makes you smile? Practices may be cognitive (i.e. regularly adopting a positive or optimistic attitude), behavioral (i.e., regularly being kind to others or regularly engaging in physical exercise) or volitional (i.e., identifying and striving for meaningful personal goals).

Sonja Lyubomrsky found preliminary support for this model of happiness. She tracked the happiness levels and life events of undergraduates over one semester and found that both life circumstances and intentional activities predicted increased happiness midway through the semester. By the end of the semester, only behavioral change predicted increased happiness. In other words, we are happy not when we are thinking about it or wishing for it but in doing it.

There is no shortcut to happiness. Happiness requires effort—sustained intentional behavior. At the end of the chapter, you will find some exercises to test this out for yourself.

HOW CAN HAPPINESS BE INCREASED?

As previously noted, there is a set point for our experience of happiness. However, there are activities we can do to increase happiness. We can raise our levels of happiness by working on three important components—getting more pleasure out of life (which can be done by savoring sensory experiences), becoming more engaged in what you do and finding a way of making your life feel more meaningful. Getting more pleasure out of life involves learning to savor the good moments of daily living: i.e., having a meal with family or friends, taking leisurely walk on the beach or in the woods, listening to some favorite music. None of these activities appeal to you? Then plan for yourself a perfect day. What would you include? Then just do it.

A significant contributor to happiness is the relationships we have. Social relationships are a powerful predictor of happiness – much more so than money. Happy people have extensive social networks and good relationships with the people in that network. For reasons of survival and satisfaction, "it is good that man should not live alone"(Genesis 1). We cannot be human alone. The Romans had a saying, "one man is no man at all." Built in us is a deep need to belong. Many of the emotional disorders that clients present at a therapist's office stem from relationship problems: difficulties in belonging, failure to have significant attachments to others or the absence of a significant other.

A few years ago Time Magazine had as its cover story, "The Science of Happiness." Reporter Claudia Wallis asked, "So what has science learned that makes the heart sing?" She found not surprisingly that our connection with others is definitely a major source of happiness. She refers to a 2002 study conducted by psychologists Diener and Seligman that found that "the most salient characteristic shared by the 10% of students with the highest levels of happiness and the fewest signs of depression were the strong ties to family and friends and commitment to spending time with them." Diener adds, "Word needs to be spread. It is important to work on social skills, close interpersonal ties, and social support in order to be happy."

Three relationship sources that either enhance or diminish happiness are friendship and marriage, kinship and involvement in spiritual and religious practices. Having a few close confiding friendships has been found to correlate with happiness and subjective wellbeing (Argyle, 2000). For example, one study of 222 college students found that the happiest 10 percent had as one of their most significant attributes a richly satisfying and full social life. They spent a significant amount of time socializing and maintaining close friendships. Why are friendships important? How do they contribute to our happiness? Here are some reasons why confiding relationships are probably associated with happiness. Close friendships provide social support. They meet needs for affiliation. They make us feel happy and satisfied. Happy people may be more often selected as friends and confidants, because they are more attractive companions than miserable people.

Folk wisdom tells us that friends can be good medicine. As a social support those with close friendships have been found to cope better with various traumas, including bereavement, rape, job loss and illness. Recently I attended a funeral of a former client. She courageously fought cancer for fifteen years. She had worked tirelessly for legislation for cancer patients who did not have health insurance at state and national levels. In reflecting on what kept her going through it all, the support of family and friends was a major factor.

MARRIAGE

Happily married people are happier than unmarried people whether they are divorced, single or never married. The unhappiest are those trapped in an unhappy marriage. The happiness gap between married and unmarried women is the same as that for men. Both men and women reap the same benefits in terms of personal happiness from marriage.

Why are married people happier? One explanation may be that happy people may be more appealing married partners. "Because they are more good-natured, more outgoing and more focused on others, they generally are more socially attractive"(Myers, p. 63). Another explanation is that marriage confers a host of benefits to make them happy. It provides psychological and physical intimacy, a context in which to have children and build a home, a social role as a spouse and parent, and a context within which to affirm identity and create posterity.

KINSHIP

Close supportive relationships between parents and children, between siblings and between extended family enhances the social support available to all family members and contributes to happiness. Maintaining such social support has physical benefits, resulting in improved immune system functioning. Such social support enhances our sense of wellbeing and from an evolutionary perspective we are "hard wired" to derive happiness from this context with our kinship networks. One of the reasons given for women outliving men is a woman's willingness to use social support. From an early age, women are socialized to be caregivers and reach out for support. Men are not. This may explain why most women who experience a death of a spouse handle the death more effectively. They know how to use their networks of support.

INVOLVEMENT IN SPIRITUAL AND RELIGIOUS ACTIVITIES

Moderate correlations have been found between involvement in religious activity and happiness (Myers, 2000). People involved in such activities may be happier than others for various reasons. One notion is that faith communities provide social support. "Where two or three are gathered together..." (Matthew, 18:20). Studies have shown that depressed individuals who are active in their faith communities have a shorter time of recovery than their non-church going counterpart. Another reason is that an actively practiced faith provides an umbrella of meaning and purpose. One researcher has contended that a loss of meaning feeds today's high depression rate and that finding meaning requires:

An attachment to something larger than the lonely self. To the extent that young people now find it hard to take seriously their relationship

17

with God, to care about their relationship with the country or to be part of a large and abiding family, they will find that it is very difficult to find meaning in life.

To put it another way, the self is a very poor site for finding meaning. (p. 55)

A third reason is that regular attendance at religious services and being a part of a religious community is often associated with a physically healthier life style characterized by marital fidelity; altruistic behavior; moderation in eating and drinking. Of all the Protestant denominations, the Seventh Day Adventists rank highest in a healthier life style for these various reasons.

In conclusion, there are activities we can do to increase our level of happiness. These daily activities should be focused on the three components of happiness: getting more pleasure out of life, becoming more engaged in what you and finding ways of making your life feel meaningful. Interestingly enough, the last two components involve a shift from a focus on self to a focus on others and causes to which we can commit ourselves. Happiness begins as an inside job, but it does not end there. Barbra Streisand had it right when she sang, "People who need people are the luckiest (*happiest*) people in the world."

Now, how about you? How happy are you? Get some idea where you are by doing the following exercises.

EXERCISES

1. Write down what activities you have participated in during the last week that were pleasurable or philanthropic. Pleasurable activities are those designed chiefly for the benefit of the self. Philanthropic activities are those that benefit others.

    a. What were the specific differences in each type of activity?

    b. What type of emotions did you feel during each type of activity?

    c.   How long did the generally positive emotions experienced during each type of activity remain with you afterward?

2. How do you define happiness in your life? What are some examples that suggest you are living the good life?

3. Measure your happiness with The Satisfaction with Life Scale devised by psychologist Ed Diener in 1980.

Read the following five statements. Then use a 1-7 scale to rate your level of Agreement

1   2   3   4   5   6   7

Not true   Moderately

Absolutely true   True

1. In most ways my life is close to my ideal.

2. The conditions of my life are excellent.

3. I am satisfied with my life.

4. So far I have gotten the important things I want in life.

5. If I could live my life over, I would change almost nothing.

Total score_____

Scoring:* 31 to 35: you are extremely satisfied with your life *26 to 30:very satisfied *21 to 25: slightly satisfied *20 is the neutral point *15 to 19: slightly dissatisfied *10 to 14: dissatisfied *5 to 9:extremely dissatisfied

2
SIGNATURE STRENGTHS
AND FL0W

The real tragedy of life is not that each of us
doesn't have enough strengths; it's that we fail
to use the ones we have.

> Donald Clifton, Ph.D.

A Gallup poll asked the following question to
managers in six countries: "Which would help you
be more successful in your life--- knowing what
your weaknesses are and attempting to improve your
weaknesses, or knowing what your strengths are and
attempting to build on your strengths?" The majority

chose to focus on improving their weaknesses. Regrettably, those who chose to build on their strengths were a minority. We are more accustomed to focusing on other's weaknesses and our own than expressing and improving our strengths.

This chapter focuses on a major emphasis of positive psychology: flow and the use of our signature strengths.

Signature strengths are those "half-dozen or so activities, mental or physical, that feel so good to do that it's almost as if you were made from them." [1] These are the skills we learn quickly, yearn to do and that energize rather than exhaust us. What are such strengths? Originality, creativity, kindness, bravery, love of learning, etc. Later in the chapter a website will be given so that you can find your signature strengths. Unlike talents, which are innate, strengths can be enhanced with practice.

Donald O. Clifton, Ph.D. is credited with focusing on discovering strengths. The American Psychological

Association named him the father of Strengths Psychology. However, many also know him as the grandfather of positive psychology. He taught psychology at the University of Nebraska. He was interested in looking at the effects of positive interactions in and out of the workplace. When you consider the fact that an estimated 22 million people are not only unhappy with their work but act out on their feelings and undermine their coworkers, you can see the necessity for changing what happens in the work arena. It is important to understand his work. Negative people love nothing more than to take others down with them. Dissatisfied employees can cost between $250 and $300 billion in lost productivity each year. His research and writings have been guided by a simple common sense notion. Instead of focusing on people's deficits, weaknesses, pathologies; focus instead on their strengths, talents and resources. A weakness orientation blinds people to their strengths that often lie dormant and neglected. Regrettably, much of psychology and psychiatry the last hundred years has been focused in this area. A quick perusal of some of the psychological labels that have worked their way into everyday conversation attests to this; "I'm not OK," adult child of alcoholic, he's schizophrenic or bipolar."

Clifton and his colleagues at The Gallup Organization asked the following question of 198,000 employees working in 7,939 business units within 36 countries: At work do you have the opportunity to do what you do best every day? They then compared the responses to the performance of the business units and discovered the following: "...when employees answered 'strongly agree' to this question, they were 50 percent more likely to work in business units with lowered employee turnover, 38 percent more likely to work in more productive units and 44 percent more likely to work in business units with higher customer satisfaction scores (p.9)

Even more startling was their discovery, after asking to this question to more than 1.7 million employees in

101 companies from 63 countries that only 20 percent of the employees surveyed felt their strengths are in play every day. Comments Clifton: "Most bizarre of all, the longer an employee stays with the organization and the higher he climbs the traditional career ladder, the less likely he is to strongly agree that he is playing to his strengths."(6)

Based on the research, Clifton believes that most organizations are built on two false assumptions about people:

1. Each person can learn to be competent in almost anything,

2. Each person's greatest room for growth is in his or her area of greatest weakness.

    Such emphases are concerned more with damage control than strength enhancement. The best managers and organizations according to Clifton are guided by two contrasting assumptions:

1. Each person's talents are enduring and unique.

2. Each person's greatest room for growth is in the areas of his or her greatest strength.

These two assumptions explain why great managers are careful to look for talent in every role and why they focus people's performance on outcomes rather than forcing them into a stylistic world.

For Clifton, strength is "consistent near perfect performance in an activity." Strength is a combination of talents, defined as naturally recurring patterns of thought, feelings or behavior, skills and knowledge. While skills and knowledge can be learned, talents are innate. For example, if you are curious, charming, responsible or competitive, these are talents.

You can begin to identify your own strengths in at least four ways. The first way is by paying close attention to your spontaneous, top-of-mind reactions to situations, and the elements that spark your interest. Think of a recent social gathering you attended. Did you get acquainted with strangers, or hang out with people you knew? If you were drawn to strangers, perhaps a genuine interest in people is one of your strengths. On the other hand, if you stuck with friends you already know, or if you hung back and didn't speak much to anyone, perhaps deep loyalty or introspection are among your strengths. All of these are useful strengths to have; none is intrinsically "better' than any of the others. It depends on how you put them to use.

If you have a weekly team strategy meeting at work, do you contribute ideas on a regular basis? If so, perhaps you have leadership skills. Do you remain quiet but interested? Maybe you are more of an implementer than a conceiver. Do you generally feel bored at your work meetings? Does your mind wander? Maybe you're in the wrong job!

Where is your mind going? THAT will tell you something about where your strengths lie. This brings us to the second approach to identifying strengths, which is to scrutinize your *yearnings*. What do you deeply yearn for, in an *abiding* way? When I say *abiding,* I mean "over a long period of time." I'm not talking here about yearning for sexual gratification or vast wealth or even relief from discomfort. Acute as such longings may be, they represent transitory desires. The type of yearning I am speaking of usually begins in childhood. What did you want to be, where did you want to be, and what did you imagine yourself doing with your life, when you were a child? Even if these early "fantasies" seem unrealistic now, they provide important hints about the direction that naturally beckons you. For example, one girl dreamed of growing up to be a detective. Though she did not ultimately pursue this goal, she finds that, as an adult, she is very observant. She watches people closely, notes their facial expressions as well as their words, and retains small details about behavior, clothing, items in a given environment, and so on. She is an outstanding judge of character. Observation and inductive reasoning are two of her major strengths.

Some things come easy to us, and others are more difficult. This is another obvious indicator of our natural abilities. Anything that is easy for us to learn, any skill that we find easy to acquire, is an area of strength. It may or may not be something we yearned for in childhood. Sometimes a talent may lie dormant for many years until it is "awakened" by a given opportunity or circumstance. One man fell in love with a woman who was an avid samba dancer. He took dancing lessons to please her, and found that he not only loved to dance, but that he learned to dance well very quickly. He discovered that dancing left him positively exhilarated in a way he'd never imagined before. As a boy growing up, he played sports, but never in his wildest dreams had he thought of himself as a dancer!

Finally, the simplest method of discovering your strengths is to identiy the activities that bring you satisfaction. What are the things you do already in your life that leave you feeling really good? Particularly in the activities that make you *happy with yourself,* you will find strong clues about your core talents.

Positive psychology research provides compelling evidence that individuals can increase their happiness by identifying and exercising their primary or "signature" strengths. A number of researchers have developed tests that can help pinpoint a person's strengths. If you are interested in zeroing in on your own strengths, and you want a little assistance, you might find these instruments helpful.

For example, Dr. Clifton developed the Strength Finder. A web-based assessment, the tool assesses normal personality from the perspective of positive psychology. There are 180 items in the Strength Finder, presented to the user over a secure connection. It analyzes your instinctive reactions and immediately presents you with your five most powerful signature strengths. While its main application has been in the work area, it is also been used for understanding individuals in a wide variety of settings. It measures thirty-four strengths that Clifton and his associates discovered during their study of excellence. Some of the strengths are Achiever, Communication, Developer, and Significance.

In an article about Clifton's work, his grandson Tom Rath lists some practical tips he learned from his grandfather for making the workplace an arena for positive interaction and improved productivity. One is the theory of the Dipper and the Bucket. "Each of us, he'd say, has an invisible bucket inside. It is filled or emptied by what people say or do to us. Full? You'll feel great! Empty? Awful! You also have an invisible dipper. You can use it to dip from others' buckets by saying or doing negative things. Or you can fill peoples' buckets by saying or doing things that increase positive emotions."

As a youngster, Tom learned the importance of giving encouragement, praise and recognition. When he was 10, Donald Clifton suggested he start some kind of business. He opened a little snack stand. The smallest accomplishment Clifton took note of. "Your first sale? That's fantastic, Tom!" By the time Tom was 12; his business employed more than 20 of his classmates. The school friends sold candy, small merchandise and apparel and got written up in the local paper. Quite an accomplishment for a 12-year old. The power of encouragement!

In a Gallup study of a major telecommunication company, the researchers were interested in discovering the employees who were able to retain customers. What made them different from the reps that scared off every single customer? They found that those who really listened to the customer and took care of the issue were the ones who retained the customer. In other words, the retainers engaged in a positive interaction with the customers.

Research on positive psychology provides compelling evidence that individuals can increase their happiness by identifying and engaging in their signature strengths. Clifton's work is one way to approach this. Another is the work of Martin Seligman and Christopher Peterson. Seligman and Peterson, a psychologist at the University of Michigan devised a web based survey instrument, Values in Action (VIA, authentichappiness.

org) an online test of 240 questions that computes a person's five "signature" strengths. Your top character traits are those that allow you to achieve meaningful happiness, instead of mere hedonistic pleasure. The list comprises 24 attributes that positive psychologists have found across cultures. The strengths are divided into six categories or virtues—wisdom and knowledge, transcendence, temperance, justice, love and courage. Each virtue contains between three and five strengths. The virtue of transcendence, for example, is broken down into the qualities of gratitude, hope, humor and beauty. It is important that you find some way to regularly put these strengths into regular practice.

For example, one of my signature strengths is *curiosity and interest in the world.* About six years ago I began learning how to play the saxophone. I am fortunate to have found an excellent teacher who introduced me to the joy, challenge, and discovery of playing that truly American art form, jazz. Learning to play jazz is a challenge intellectually and emotionally.

Each day's practice satisfies my need for curiosity and challenge. One never does arrive. It was reported that saxophone great John Coltrane at the height of his fame used to practice between sets at various jazz clubs!

Betty Rodriquez, a family therapist-turned coach, says her awareness of her strengths helped her cope with the sudden death of her parents a year ago. Her mother and stepfather were killed in a traffic accident in Tennessee. In the days that followed, she comforted herself by expressing one of her signature strengths-- appreciation of beauty and excellence—when writing her mother's obituary. At the funeral she consciously tried to use gratitude: her third signature strength. "I went up to everyone I knew, thanked them for coming, and told them my parents would have been so honored that they were there," she says. "It made me feel strong."

David E. Mullen, Ph.D.

FLOW AND USING OUR
SIGNATURE STRENGTHS

When we use our signature strengths, we are more likely to experience *flow*. Dr. Mihaly Csikszentmihalyi is a professor of psychology at Claremont Graduate Institute. He is credited with defining the term. By flow he means full engagement with our experience. When we are engaged in challenging but controllable tasks that are intrinsically motivating we experience a unique psychological state, referred to as flow. Almost any activity can produce flow if these elements are present. Making them a constant part of your life can enhance your work, personal relationships and leisure time.

Csikszentmihalyi has studied the lives of thousands of people for more than 30 years in search of what makes people's lives meaningful and satisfying. He has found that most people live at two extremes—they are stressed by work or obligations or they are bored by spending their leisure time on activities such as watching television. But, he says, people can live richer, happier lives by learning new skills and increasing the challenges they face each day. "A typical day is full of anxiety and boredom," says Csikszentmihalyi. "Flow experiences provide the flashes of intense living against this dull background."

He writes: "The metaphor of flow is one that many people have used to describe the sense of effortless action they feel in moments that stand out as the best in their lives. Athletes refer to it as 'being in the zone,' religious mystics as being in 'ecstasy,' artists and musicians call it aesthetic rapture."

On August 22, 1741, George Frederic Handel shut the door, sat down at his keyboard, picked up a quill, and began to compose. Twenty-four days and nights later, he emerged with 260 ink-filled pages, some of them streaked from his own tears. The result came fully to life on April 13, 1742, at Dublin's New Music

Hall, with the debut of the majestic oratorio now known to the world as "Messiah."

Recalling the creation of his two-and-a-half-hour masterpiece, Handel told a friend, "Whether I was in the body or out of my body when I wrote it, I know not." He worked nonstop, frequently skipping meals. The effort so captured his heart that he often wept as the music flowed. After composing the section known as the "Hallelujah Chorus," he wrote in his journal, "I think I did see all Heaven before me and the great God himself."

Flow states can be contrasted with the anxiety and pressure many of us feel to meet our obligations or the passive boredom we feel when in leisure situations. Flow occurs when our highest signature strengths meet the challenge of a high-risk situation.

The opposite states of flow are either anxiety or boredom. Flow is a powerful antidote to the trance-like states many people experience. The Russian philosopher

Guardejeff described such people as sleepwalkers; hypnotized automatons that needed to wake-up.

There are a number of factors that must be present in order to experience flow. We must have a good chance of completing the tasks. There must be clear goals and immediate feedback. We experience flow when we are completely engaged in a task. Our sense of time changes. In fact, we lose a sense of time. Our self is so absorbed in the task that our sense of self disappears. Paradoxically, the sense of self emerges after the task is completed.

Through his research, Csikzentmihalyi has found that some activities more than others lend themselves to an experience of flow: reading, sailing, chess, rock climbing, dancing, writing and group motorcycling. Passive activities such as watching TV or a movie do not. One of the distinguishing marks of the flow activities is that they become ends in themselves. These experiences are said to be 'autotelic'. The word comes from the Greek words self (auto) and goal (telos).

Autotelic experiences are those that arise from activities, which are not done for some anticipated future benefit but because the activity in itself is intrinsically and immediately rewarding. For example, a writer describes getting lost in her writing. A musician gets so absorbed in playing a composition he loses track of time. An individual engages in a stimulating conversation and later he wonders where the time has gone.

Flow experiences have been applied to work and relationships. Work-based flow experiences are more common in cultures that permit people to have work roles that are neither monotonously boring nor overly challenging and stressful, but where role demands meet workers' skill level. Mark Strand, former poet laureate of the United States describes the experience of flow well: "You're right in the work, you lose your sense of time, you're completely caught up in what you are doing...when you are working on something and you're working well, you have the feeling that there's no other way of saying what you are saying." Flow experiences are not the sole province of writers, athletes, and musicians. The assembly line worker, the businessman, the housewife, and the mentor can also experience them. They are individuals who work differently. It is not the external conditions that determine how much work will contribute to the excellence of one's life. It is how one works and what experiences one is able to derive from confronting its challenges.

EXERCISES

1. Compose a one page positive introduction to yourself. Don't be modest! Let the introduction tell a concrete story that shows you at your best and illustrates your highest strengths. Give the story a beginning, a middle and a strong ending.

2. Discover your signature strengths by taking the test on authentichappiness.org.

3
OPTIMISM

It's as though there were two attorneys in your mind, one gathering evidence for "Life is Awful" and the other gathering evidence for "Life is Wonderful." You're the judge and can rule out any evidence you want. Your decision is final. Which judicial ruling do you suppose would lead to more joy, happiness, peace, and ease? [1]

As children, many of us were read the story, The Little Engine That Could." It is a tale of a little engine that was called upon to take a heavy load of materials up a rugged and treacherous mountain. The other larger engines were either out of the train yard or out of commission. The challenge fell to the little engine. Remember his words as he took up the challenge: "I think I can. I think I can. I think I can." It became his mantra. He was displaying optimism.

What does positive psychology tell us about the importance of optimism? What is its effect on health, relationships, success in business, etc.? How can you raise an optimistic child? If you are a pessimist, can you become more optimistic?

What is optimism? Psychologically, optimism is the tendency to seek out, remember and expect pleasurable experiences. It is an active priority of the person, not merely a reflex that prompts us to look at the bright side.

Seven-year-old Kealan Jewell is positive about everything. She unabashedly declares she is one of the most popular girls in her class. When asked what she wants to be when she grows up, she doesn't think twice.

"I'm going to be an artist," she says, "I'd like to write a book, but can't find the time." [2]

Keelan is an optimist—as are most children her age. So was the American philosopher Henry Thoreau, who used to lie in bed in the mornings for a few minutes thinking positive thoughts. He would remind himself that he was healthy, that his mind was alert, that his work was interesting, that the future looked bright and that many people trust him. When he got out of bed, he entered a world filled with the kind of positive, good people and opportunities that he expected—a kind of self-fulfilling prophecy.

EXPLANATORY STYLE

One of the ways to determine whether we are an optimist or pessimist is to look at what psychologists call our explanatory style. That is, how we explain to ourselves a negative event. Everyone's explanatory style can be coded on three dimensions: *personal ("me – not me"), permanent ("always – not always"), pervasive ("everything-not everything").*

Consider the following scenario. Frank, Steven and Cindy make a sales presentation after weeks of preparation. The response from the new manager, "Lousy! You've completely missed the boat."

Look at their different responses. Frank gets ANGRY. And rages about his boss. "He doesn't know anything about the client or this product. He hates everything I do. I could do his job better than he does. It's not fair." Doing work becomes more and more difficult and Frank develops frequent stomach pains.

Steven WORRIES. "I knew he wouldn't understand what I was trying to do," he thinks. "I don't fit here anymore. I'll probably be fired soon. I'll never get anything right. I'm a failure." Steven finds it harder to go to the office in the morning can't concentrate on his work and has trouble sleeping.

Cindy feels DISAPPOINTED at first then CHALLENGED. "He certainly sees things differently,

" she reflects, "I'd better find out what he was expecting." Cindy sets up a meeting with her boss to discuss revisions of the presentation.

Frank, Steven, and Cindy each interpreted the same event in different ways and each one had different feelings, actions, and consequences. Let's look in more detail at the specifics of each response.

Frank and Steven see the setback ("lousy presentation") as PERMANENT. "He (the boss) hates everything I do." "I'll never get anything right. I'll be fired,"thinks Stephen.

On the other hand, Cindy views the setback as TEMPORARY. "He certainly sees things differently," thinks Cindy.

Now Frank and Steven also view the setback in GLOBAL terms. "I'll never get anything right. He hates everything I do."

Cindy sees the setback in SPECIFIC terms. "I'd better find out what he was expecting." In contrast, Frank and Steven explained the comments by blaming themselves. They internalized the boss's comments. "I'm a failure."

What has just been described is one way of looking at the difference between an optimistic versus a pessimistic explanation of bad events. According to this perspective, optimistic people explain negative events or experiences by attributing the causes to transient, specific, external factors. Pessimists explain negative events or experiences by attributing the causes to stable, global and internal factors. For example, optimists are more likely to say they failed an exam because the wrong questions came up or the atmosphere in the exam room was not conducive to concentration. Pessimists, in contrast, are more likely to attribute failure to not being any good at academic work generally or to being stupid.

Let's find out if you are an optimist or pessimist. Do you agree or disagree with the following statements? Don't respond with what you think you SHOULD say, but how you typically view your life.

In uncertain times I expect the best.

I always look on the bright side.

I'm optimistic about my future.

Every cloud has a silver lining.

If something can go wrong it will.

Things never work out the way I want them to.

I rarely count on good things happening to me.

If you agree with the first four statements and disagree with the last three, you are an optimist. If you disagree with the first four statements and agree with the last three, you are more pessimistic.

These items are part of an inventory, "The Life Orientation Test," developed by Michael Shier, professor of psychology at Carnegie Mellon University.

The most common quality of optimists is that they see good in situations and truly expect things to go their way. Anticipating a favorable outcome leads an optimist to do things that actually determine the final outcome. Optimists expect things to turn out well, but they can also do things that change the course of events. Put another way, optimists see events in their life for the most part as controllable. When something bad happens, optimists are not defeated. Instead, they make a plan of action and follow it. They expect they will be able to handle anything that comes along and they are usually right.

Now this optimism is not a 'whistling in the dark," or a forced cheerfulness; optimists express acceptance or resignation when needed. University of Miami psychologist Charles Carver says that researchers "don't mean to imply that people should put on a happy face and go around being mindlessly cheerful all the time. Even optimists have occasional doubts or fail sometimes. By resignation, we mean the ability to say, "I'm not going to pretend this isn't happening but if I have to put up with it, I will."[3]

However it is measured, optimism does appear to play a role in good health. It has what statisticians call a "modest correlation" between explanatory styles and health. When you factor in the other many factors that contribute to physical well-beings, such as genetics, environment, diet, exercise, and environmental hazards, a moderate correlation can have an important effect.

In a series of studies, optimism was found linked to good heath and pessimism to poor health. For example, pessimistic undergraduates developed more physical symptoms over times than their optimistic counterparts, even when they started out equally. In another study, dispositional optimism—the degree to which someone expects the future to bring positive events rather than negative ones—predicted how well men recovered six months after undergoing bypass surgery. Compared to pessimistic patients, the optimists were more likely to have returned to work and resumed recreational, social, and sexual activities. They were also more likely to be exercising vigorously. [4]

Chris Peterson at the University of Michigan studied the relationship between explanatory style and physical health among 172 undergraduates at Virginia Tech. They completed three questionnaires: one measured optimism; another looked for depressive symptoms; and the third had the students describe all the illnesses they have experienced during the previous 30 days. For each illness they reported the date they first noticed symptoms and the last day they felt them. The degree of illness was then calculated, based on the number of days that at least one symptom was present. One month later, the students were questioned about any illnesses they had experienced during the 30 days since they had completed the questionnaire. Finally, they were contacted one year later and asked the number of times they had visited a physician during the past year for diagnosis or treatment of any illness. The study found that college students with an optmisitic explanatory style had fewer days of illness in the subsequent month and made fewer doctor visits in the subsequent year than did their more pessimistic peers. These results held even when the subjects' initial health status and level of depression (since depressed people might complain more) were factored in. [5]

In a similar study, researchers found the optimistic students reported fewer ills. Pessimists, as a rule, care less about their health. In addition, pessimists blame themselves for their failure but then do little to improve their lot. Optimists, on the other hand, view failures as problems that can be fixed. They meet their problems head on, form a plan of action and achieve results. [6]

What are the limits of optimism? Optimistic attitudes are certainly not always the major factor in determining who gets sick and who stays well. Your genetic inheritance, smoking, diet, nutrition, environmental conditions, and other factors play a role. Sometimes biological factors dominate, and no amount of positive thinking will reverse them. Still, optimistic thinking can help you to prevent some illnesses and cope better with others. Healthy thinking may not prolong your survival, but it can help you maximize your health and functioning in the meantime.

OPTIMISM, MENTAL HEALTH AND PERFORMANCE

Besides its effect on physical health, optimism has been studied in relation to mental health and performance. Writing about some of the great entrepreneurs of our day, *Success* editor Scott DeGarno wrote, "Learning how to rebound with optimism is part of adapting to a world of constant change. Optimism is one of the key characteristics of the men and women who make a difference."

Perseverance is the fuel that keeps optimists performing. Optimists keep at it; pessimists give up and fail, even if they have equal talent. And because optimists are always hopeful about the outcome, they tend to take more risks and try out new things.

Dr. Martin Seligman has demonstrated that optimists are more successful and perform better than pessimists in almost all fields—business, education, sports and politics. For example, he convinced insurance giant

Metropolitan Life that in selecting agents, optimism should be a key factor. He developed a twenty-minute written exam to screen the applicants. The exam separated the optimists from the pessimists and Met Life hired a new sales force based on measured optimism. By the end of the first year, the optimistic sales force was outselling the others by 20 percent. By the end of the second year, they were outselling the others by 50 percent

Want to become more optimistic? Psychologist Christopher Peterson states that a good choice to make is an area that is important enough to demand attention and concern but not so critical that the thought of change frightens you into inaction. Choose an area of life in which to become more optimistic: perhaps work or family or friends or the future or health. Here are some ways to boost your optimism:

1. Realize you may need to make a lifestyle change.

2. Start small by choosing one area of your life in which to become more optimistic and then become aware of the way you think in relation to that area.

3. Take a good, hard critical look at your beliefs about yourself and about that area of your life: How realistic are they?

4. Set goals that are small enough to achieve quickly. Then reward yourself when you meet those goals. It's important to reward yourself when you reach even the most modest goal.

5. Seek out optimistic people; seek a good friend.

6. Play at being optimistic; stay flexible. [7]

EXERCISES:

1. Rehearse success. When you aren't happy with the way you handled a particular situation, try this exercise:

* Write down three ways it could have gone better.

* Write down three ways it could have gone worse.

* If you can't think of alternatives to the way you handled it, imagine what someone whom you greatly respect would have done.

* Or think what advice you would give to someone facing a similar situation.

4
HOPE

"I've got high hopes…high hopes…"

Words & Music by Sammy Cahn & Jimmy

Van Heusen Sung by Frank Sinatra

President Reagan was fond of telling jokes and stories. One of my favorites was his story of the two boys on the farm. They each had a job to do. One was driving a shiny tractor, plowing the field for spring planting. The other boy had the job of cleaning out the animal stalls. Later in the morning the boy on the tractor sees that his friend is smiling while he is doing his job. Curious, he asks his friend, "You have the worst of the two jobs and yet you are smiling. Why?" Quipped the friend, " Well, with all this horse manure, there is got to be a pony somewhere!" That boy had high hopes. He is an optimist.

In his masterful book on the history of psychotherapy *Persuasion And Healing*, Dr. Jerome Frank traces the history of healing from ancient healers, priests, witchdoctors, and shamans to the modern day psychotherapist. Despite their different rituals and orientations, the common thread running through them all is the offering of hope to the sufferer. Without hope, the future indeed looks bleak and dark. One of the major symptoms of someone contemplating suicide is hopelessness; the attitude that life will not be different.

We could all agree that hope is important to one's subjective well-being and happiness. But what is hope and how does positive psychology view it? Hope is a way of approaching life that says "yes" and "I can," Hope is future-minded. It helps us look at our goals;

how we may move toward these goals and how we deal with barriers or obstacles to these goals.

C. R. Snyder, professor of psychology at the University of Kansas, is one of the leading researchers in the area of hope and provides an interesting way to understand it. He views hope as an active process that includes three components: goal, will power, and way power. How people think about their goals determines how they move toward them.

A *goal* is something you desire to do or to have. Perhaps you want to lose 10 pounds for the upcoming high school reunion or you want to get into shape for next year's marathon. Or you are a young couple who wants to buy your first home or a baby boomer who wants to have enough money for a comfortable retirement. As you can see, a goal can be a variety of things, large or small, that we actively work toward.

A second component of hope is *way power*. This is our capacity to develop ways to meet our goals. It is the ability to find different routes when a road is closed.

To demonstrate way power, let's see what happens to Chris who has decided to make an Italian meal for the family. Now Chris is good on the grill and enjoys barbecuing chicken and grilling steaks. However, he has not made many Italian dishes. After selecting a tasty Italian recipe, he mixes the ingredients and preheats the oven. When he is ready to add the vinegar, he finds that he is a half cup short. Chris has a couple of options. He could go to the friendly supermarket and buy the vinegar, or perhaps he could send his teenage daughter to the store. He, or his daughter, could also go next door and borrow the vinegar, which he decides to do. Chris is demonstrating way power when he discerns the several ways he could get the vinegar he needs to finish the dish—his goal.

Will power, the third component of hope, is the driving force in hopeful things. It is the energy that propels us toward our goal(s). It is the internal self-talk such as "I can do it," I think I can," or "I can do this."

This energy is not outside us: it comes from within. We draw on it to move toward the goal that is our focus.

Think of it this way. The goal is the target, whether large or small. Way power is the way we move toward the goal. Will power is the energy that keeps us moving.

When thinking about will power, remember Rosa Parks, the activist, who became a symbol for the Civil Rights Movement when she refused to sit in the back of that Montgomery, Alabama bus in 1955. While we do not know her inner thoughts, the day that Rosa Parks sat in the front of the bus she must have been driven by the energy of her desire for freedom and told herself she could make a stand. Or consider St. Louis Cardinal batter, Mark McGuire, who put so much mental and physical energy into his home run records in the 1998 baseball season.

Will power does not have to be in such extreme proportions as demonstrated by these national figures.

Everyone has will power. I think of a woman I know who was given only a few months to live. She refused to take the doctor's prognosis as the final word. Her goal was to be well enough to attend her daughter's upcoming wedding and spend some one-on-one time with her son who was being deployed to the war in Iraq. She actively sought other medical opinions. She surrounded herself with a network of loving and compassionate friends and was an active participant in her healing. She was able to realize her hope. Her illness is in remission.

Like its cousin, optimism, hope includes an important cognitive aspect: self-talk. Self-talk is an important part of the process of hope. What one tells oneself about the process has everything to do with the realization of the goal. Cognitive psychology states that a person's core cognitions play an important role in motivating behavior. What we tell ourselves affects how we feel and how we behave. And important aspect of self-talk is the internalized message we have received from important people in our life. People become low in hope as a result of self-defeating messages they heard and internalized when young. This includes not only the parental behavior we observed as children: how they dealt with successes, set-backs, and frustrations in meeting their goals; but also the family stories they told us became a part of the learnings we draw upon. Such stories are influential. These stories live in us, often without our being aware of it. Consider the difference that the following stories might have on a person's becoming a hopeful person: stories of courage and determination or messages that it's a dog-eat dog world. Consider, too, how positive or negative statements by significant others to the growing child can enhance or diminish the capacity for hopefulness. For examples, "You can do it" versus "You will never amount to much." One helpful exercise is to write a few family stories you have been told and look at the themes of these stories. Are they full of hope or are they full of defeat and disappointment?

Many years ago CBS personality Walter Cronkite interviewed Eric Hoffer, the blind San Francisco longshoreman who quit school in the eighth grade. As an adult he wrote the influential book, *The True Believer.* Cronkite asked him to describe the source of his inspiration. Without hesitation, Hoffer stated, "My mother. She believed in me." This is a reminder of what Snyder's research has demonstrated that hope is learned through examples set by people important to us.

Civil Rights Activist and Nobel Prize winner Dr. Martin Luther King, Jr. related a time in his life during the civil rights struggle when he was very despondent and ready to give up. His life had been threatened numerous times, he had been jailed, he feared for the safety of his family. Windows of his home had been shattered numerous times by strangers in the night. He gathered with his followers at the home of a dear friend, Mother Pollard, where he shared his distress and vulnerability. At that meeting, as he later reported,

Mother Pollard listened intently to him and then walked toward him. Putting her hands on his shoulders in that hushed room, she said, "You can't give up the fight. God is with us. He will give us the strength to go on." Her words were like rain on a parched desert, food for his soul. Her words of encouragement gave him new hope and resolve. Never underestimate the power of encouragement to us by significant others in reaching our goals!

We also need to encourage ourselves. We need to be our own best coaches and cheerleaders. Such self-encouragement is especially needed when one faces obstacles and barriers toward reaching one's goals. The sense of personal agency - "I think I can" - helps the person to apply the needed motivation to seek the best alternate pathway.

THE DEVELOPMENT OF HOPE

Having discussed the importance of internalized messages in the disposition to have high or low hope, we now turn the attention to how hope develops. How does hope grow? I return to Snyder's study on hope for insight. By the end of the first year of life, the infant is attached to a dependable significant other and begins to see that her actions have consequences. For example, the infant is able to point toward an object she wants.

In the second year, infants learn to engage in goal-directed activities to follow pathways to desired goals. An important hope-producing skill learned during this period is how to handle and effectively deal with frustrations and barriers. Herein lies the genesis of hope: the development of the sense of an active self that can effectively deal with barriers

During the later preschool years (ages 3 to 6) when the child is developing language and physical skills, she continues to grow in hopeful planning in the face of obstacles. A crucial ingredient for this to happen is the relationship between the child and the caregiver. Children who are securely attached to their caregivers and are provided with sufficient support to cope with adversity develop resilience and hope.

In adolescence, youngsters develop abstract reasoning skills. These skills become critical in the management of relationships, consideration of career paths, and separation from parents as they grow into adulthood. These issues provide opportunities for the hopeful planning and pursuit of goals despite setbacks.

In adulthood, individuals high in hope deal with adversity differently than those low in hope. High hope adults experience as many setbacks as others in their lives, but they see these problems as challenges. Internal self-talk is the key. "I can do it." "I will not give up." Thomas Edison failed over 150 times before he found the right filament for the light bulb. When asked about these "failures," he commented, "These were not failures; they were mistakes. Each one led me closer to discovering the correct one." These affirmations are part of the internal dialogue of such individuals. Emotionally, when facing a significant barrier, the adult with high hope experiences less negative emotions, probably because of their capacity to develop alternative pathways to their goal. When the adult with low hope faces a similar frustration, they are likely to use counter-productive ways of coping, such as catastrophizing or avoidance. Their emotions range from rage to despair to apathy. This coping style is linked to distress and decreased functioning when used over the long run.

THE BENEFITS OF HOPE

There is a growing body of studies that demonstrates that hope is good for our psychological and physical well-being. For example, children, adolescents, and adults with higher levels of hope do better in school and athletics, have better health, have better problem solving skills, and are more adjusted psychologically. 3

In a 6-year longitudinal study, Hope Scale Scores taken at the beginning of student's very first semester in college predicted higher cumulative grade point average and graduation rate as well as lower attrition (as measured by dropout rate). Studies of college track athletes with high as compared with low hope perform significantly better in their events. In terms of hope and physical health, there is a small but growing amount of research that supports the concept that hopeful thinking is related to activities that help to prevent physical illness. People with high hope use information about physical illness to their advantage. They are more likely to engage in regular exercise programs. More specifically, high hope has been linked to benefits in dealing with spinal cord injuries, burns, fibromylagia, and blindness.

PSYCHOLOGICAL BENEFITS

Stress is an inescapable part of life. The ways in which we cope with the demands of life have important psychological and physical implications. Coping is defined as the ability to respond to a stressor(s) so as to reduce psychological (and physical) pain. Hope plays an important role in coping. Remember that the working definition of hope is the ability to use pathways to desired goals, despite obstacles and the agency or motivation to use these pathways. In other words, the high hope individual says, "yes" to these demands of living, and confidently moves toward his goals. Higher hope people produce more strategies for dealing with the stressor and express a greater likelihood of using these strategies.

EXERCISES

1. Write a one-page narrative about some of the stories you were told as a child. Look for the

messages regarding hope or its absence contained with them. These stories are important because they often become the lens through which we view goals and obstacles.

2. Think of a valued goal you want to achieve, i.e., stopping smoking, losing weight, reducing debt load, getting along better with your teenager. Meet with people who have accomplished your goal successfully and ask them to tell you the ways that worked for them.

3. Identify a goal you have reached recently and describe the steps you went through as you worked for it.

   a. Roadblocks I encountered were _____

   b. The methods I used to cope with the roadblocks were _____

   c. The thoughts I used to cope with the roadblocks were _____

   d. The outcome was _____

5
GRATITUDE

I hear babies cry, I watch them grow.

They'll learn much more than I'll ever know

And I think to myself

What a Wonderful World.

Yes, I think to myself,

What a Wonderful World.

       Words and Music by George D. Weiss &

            George Douglas.

     Recorded by Louis Årmstrong, 1967

This song made popular by Louis Årmstrong is a

hymn of gratitude, one person's appreciation and delight

in simply being alive in the world. Whether listening to his records or seeing him in person as I did in college, I was struck by the joy I felt in his presence. I don't think it was fake. Årmstrong was a person who appreciated and delighted in being in the world, and his gratitude was contagious. Åfter you left one of his concerts, you stepped a little lighter, had a smile on your face and looked at others with greater appreciation.

In spite of the fact that gratitude is an important human emotion and its presence combats stress and leads to a harmonious life, psychologists have only recently studied it. For years, gratitude was thought to be exclusively a moral disposition and virtue. Most of the major spiritual traditions treated gratitude as a basic and desirable aspect of human life. Gratitude is viewed as a highly prized human character strength in Jewish, Christian, Muslim, Buddhist, and Hindu thought. Christian writers such as Thomas a Kempis, Thomas Åquinas, and Bernard of Clairvaus wrote on the virtues of gratitude and the sinfulness of ingratitude. The

73

medieval Christian mystic Meister Eckhart suggests that if the only prayer we say in our lifetime is "thank you," that would suffice.

Positive psychology lists gratitude as a character strength and has developed assessment tools to measure its place in the well-lived life.

GRATITUDE: A DEFINITION

What is gratitude? The word comes from the Latin gratis, which means grace, graciousness, and gratefulness. Gratitude is the subjective sense of wonder and appreciation for the gift of life. When we are grateful, we are thankful for being recipients of the gifts and kindnesses of others.

A distinction can be made between personal gratitude and what psychologist Robert Emmons calls transpersonal gratitude. Personal gratitude is the thankfulness toward another person for the benefits that the person has provided. Transpersonal gratitude is gratefulness to God, a higher power, or the cosmos.

This transpersonal gratitude is akin to what psychologist Abraham Maslow called a peak experience, a moment of profound gratefulness. He writes:

People during and after peak experiences characteristically feel lucky, fortunate. A common reaction is "I don't deserve this." Å common consequence is a feeling of gratitude in religious persons, to their God; in others, to fate or nature or to just good fortune. This can go over into worship, giving thanks, adoring, giving praise, oblation, and other reactions, which fit easily into an orthodox framework. [1]

Typically, gratitude leads to a warm sense of appreciation for somebody or something, and a desire to act that flows from that. Gratitude, then, is a response to another's generosity.Why is gratitude important? One notion is that gratitude is a moral affect---that is, one with moral precursors and consequences. By experiencing gratitude, we are often motivated to carry out positive behavior toward others; we are energized to sustain moral behaviors and inhibited from committing destructive interpersonal behaviors. When we are grateful, we want to pass it on. For example, you have car trouble—you have a flat tire or your car stops abruptly. A stranger stops and offers to help. You offer to pay the person for their trouble. They refuse. Their response? Pass it on by helping another motorist in trouble.

I remember a particularly difficult in my life, dealing with the illness of a family member and mounting financial pressures. I was sharing this struggle one day with my brother. He listened very carefully and then wrote me a check. I had not asked for money. His generosity touched me, and I was at a loss for words. His response to my gratitude was, "that's what family is for." I still remember the love and warmth I felt in my appreciation of his kindness and generosity. Since then, I have tried to help others who have been in need, remembering my brother's generosity to me.

CONSEQUENCES OF GRATITUDE

Oprah introduced many to the power of living thankfully and keeping track of one's blessings in a gratitude journal. Researchers also have studied individuals who kept gratitude journals. They found that expressing gratitude has important physical and psychological benefits:

1. Those who kept such journals exercised more regularly, reported fewer physical symptoms, felt better about their lives, and were more optimistic about the upcoming week, compared with those who recorded hassles or neutral life events.

2. Grateful people report having higher levels of positive emotions, life satisfaction,

vitality, and optimism, and they have lower levels of depression and stress.

3. The disposition toward gratefulness tends to increase good feelings more than it diminishes unpleasant emotions.

4. Grateful people were more likely to help someone with a personal problem or offer emotional support to another.

5. Those who are regular church members who pray and read religious material are likely to be more grateful

6. Grateful people are less prone to place undue emphasis on material possessions, less likely to judge their own and other's success in terms of material possessions accumulated. They are less envious of wealthy persons. One of my favorite stories that illustrate the importance of giving thanks, is from Robert Coles' 1987 article, "The Power of Prayer", in *50 Plus*. It concerns a seventy-six year old

Spanish-speaking man who lives in a small village north of Santa Fe, New Mexico. He describes the essential rhythms of his life in this way:

For us the day begins with a prayer of thanks to God, for giving us another day here. And in the evening, when we go to bed, we stop and say thank you, dear Lord, for the gift of another day with our children and grandchildren. It is only a few moments any of us is here, we know—because life goes on and on, and we are but one stalk of corn, and many stalks are planted and grown and are harvested season after season. But the one who puts us here and then gathers us up—He is the one who should hear from us with a please, a thank you, a wave, a smile. If we cry, He'd like to know why. If we are happy. He'd like to know why. It's not right to think you're the lord and master of this place. He is the one who has His eyes on us and wants the best for us.

Some research suggests that gratefulness as an attitude underlies successful functioning in the life cycle. In a longitudinal study of male adult development, psychiatrist George Vallant studied men who graduated from Harvard from 1945 – 1985. He was interested in such things as their professional and personal successes and failures, the state of their physical, mental, and emotional health—their overall adaptation to life. What separated those who were able to effectively adapt from those who did not? One of his conclusions was that if they let their resentments and grievances go, they were able to be at peace with themselves and with other people.

HOW GRATITUDE DEVELOPS

We do not know much about how gratitude develops in children. What is known is that before age 6, gratitude does not appear regularly in response to receiving benefits. Before age 6, children are quite egocentric. They believe the world revolves around them and people exist to meet their every need and want. "I want what I want and I want it now!" is the attitude. In their world gratitude does not exist. How can you be grateful if you believe that people are around simply to meet your needs? One study found that about 21% of children younger than 6 years of age, expressed thanks to adults who gave them candy, whereas most children, more than 80% of a group 10 years of age or older, expressed gratitude in the same situation.

Since children 10 years old and up are capable of learning gratitude, some schools have taken the lead in developing a climate that educates children to express gratitude. They use blessing journals in which they reflect on what they are thankful for and how they can express gratitude. For example, The Thanksgiving Leadership Forum of Dallas, composed of business and civic leaders, sponsors an essay writing contest for high school students in which they write a 1,000-word essay on gratitude. College scholarships are awarded for the best essays.

THE GRATEFUL HEART

How can we cultivate a grateful heart? Some factors would include optimism, a generous outlook on life and a genuine spirituality. To feel grateful, we need to recognize our connectedness to others. "No man is an island unto himself," stated poet John Donne. When we are grateful, we realize that life is a gift and we are the recipients of the kindnesses of others.

Gratitude is more than a feeling; it is an attitude. Obviously there are situations in life where it would be very difficult to feel grateful—being laid off from a job, a child having trouble in school, an ill parent or loved one. Should we feel grateful in these situations? Of course not. Even though we may have a grateful attitude toward life, we may or may not feel grateful.

That is, OUR FEELINGS ARE NOT UNDER OUR CONTROL. ONLY OUR ATTITUDE IS. The attitude is gratitude.

Brother David Stindal-Rast, who has written extensively on gratefulness, reminds us that a grateful attitude reflects a basic and deep trust in life. Despite whatever difficulties we may face, a grateful attitude is a stance that we deliberately take. Gratefulness affirms that at its depths, there is a basic goodness in life. Albert Einstein put it this way, "Is the Universe friendly or not?" How we answer that question determines whether we will be grateful.

I have been privileged to learn about gratitude and living from working with the dying. It is a sacred work. They have taught me a lot about what really matters. I will never forget a woman whom I will call Janet. She was my patient for a couple of years. She was struggling with cancer. Earlier in her life she had successfully gotten through other serious health and family problems, but this time she was not as fortunate, and she had only a few months to live. During those last weeks, I would either call her or see her every few days. We would often have tea on her back porch. She would walk me through her garden pointing out the beautiful daffodils or lilacs she had planted. She also had a precious cat that I had grown to be fond of and she delighted in feeding her while we talked. What struck me was her deep appreciation for the moments and minutes. She was grateful for each precious breath she took.

The majority of dying patients I have sat with and listened to were grateful people. Grateful for the precious gift of each day, relationships, a sunny day or fresh-cut flowers on the table. What a paradox! People keenly aware of their dying were appreciative of their everyday blessings. When a man is dying, he does not lament that he should have worked harder or amassed more creature comforts or wish that he could have been a Donald Trump or Bill Gates. No, it is more likely that he will regret that he did not spend more time with loved ones or friends, take more walks in the woods or at the beach, or told his loved ones what they mean to him. I am reminded of a Jewish saying that death is important because it reminds us that our lives are limited and therefore, precious.

Many of us read Thornton Wilder's classic play, "Our Town," in high school. One of the most moving and powerful scenes in the play is at the end, Emily's colloquy. She is granted her wish to go back home to Grover's Corners, New Hampshire. She sees her parents and friends who have died. She sees the landmarks of the town, the church, the town meeting hall, and other sights She reminisces about them and then asks, "Does anyone ever realize how wonderful life is when you are living it?"

One important way to appreciate and be grateful for our life is to be open to wonder and surprise. Have you ever noticed how your eyes open a bit wider when you are surprised? It is as if you had been asleep, merely daydreaming, or sleepwalking through some routine activity, and then you hear your favorite tune on the radio, or look up from the middle of the parking lot and see a rainbow, or the telephone rings and it is the voice of an old friend. And all of a sudden you're awake! Often looking back, we can see these surprises as a gift.

Surprises help gratefulness to grow. If a surprise happens when something unexpected shows up, let's not expect anything at all. In her poem "Expect Nothing," Alice Walker put it this way: "Expect nothing. Live frugally on surprise."

Once we stop taking things for granted, surprise and gratefulness can develop. For example, think of the marvels of technology—the computer, the cell phone, TV, electric ignitions that turn on our car with a simple turn of the key. More amazing are our bodies. Two simple examples. Your body both produces and destroys 15 million red blood cells every second. Fifteen million! That's nearly twice the census figures for New York City. The blood vessels in your body, if lined up end to end, would reach around the world. Yet your heart needs only one minute to pump your blood through this filigree network and back again. It's been doing so, minute-by-minute, day-by-day, for the past number of years you've been alive and it still keeps pumping away at 100,000 heartbeats every 24 hours. Unfortunately, many of us take our bodies for granted and pay little attention to them until a breakdown occurs.

What blocks the grateful heart? A sense of entitlement, preoccupation with materialism, and a lack of self-reflection create some of the factors. The enemy of gratefulness is narcissism. Narcissism takes its name from Greek mythology. Narcissus was a handsome young man who was so absorbed with his image that he drowned in a pond looking at his reflection. People with narcissistic tendencies have a strong sense of entitlement: they should receive special privileges and rights. They believe they are special. Their motto: I am the greatest and better than anybody else. They are like a character described in a novel, "Edith was small country bound by the North, South, East, and West by Edith." Narcissists are exceedingly selfish and demanding. Such an attitude leads to manipulating people. Instead of loving people and using things, the narcissist loves things and uses people. Why are they so ungrateful? Gratitude researcher Robert Emmons provides an answer, "If one is entitled to everything, then one is thankful for nothing."

In conclusion, gratitude is our heartfelt response to the generosity and kindnesses of others. It is our statement that we are all interconnected. Our lives are lived in a network of relationships. When we offer thanks, we affirm this.

EXERCISES

To increase your sense of gratitude, experiment with the following exercises.

1. Perform five random acts of kindness per week. Choose acts of kindness that meet

two criteria: (1) the act benefits another person and (2) the act requires you to give something away (i.e., your time, your energy, your food or some other personal resource). Psychologist Sonja Lyubomirsky found that such activities trigger a cascade of positive effects—it makes you feel generous and capable, gives you a greater sense of connection with others and wins you smiles, approval and reciprocated kindness.

2. Write down three good things (big or small) that happened during the day every night for one week. Next to each good thing noted, answer the question, "Why did this good thing happen?"

3. Do a "gratitude visit." Think of some one who has shown you kind ness and made a difference in your life. Now write a gratitude letter to that person. Make it concrete and specific. Then call that person and ask to

visit. Don't say why (surprise is essential). Read the letter aloud, showing and making eye contact. (Exercises 2 and 3 adapted from Martin Seligman)

6
FORGIVENESS

If we could read the secret history of our enemies,
we should find in each person's life sorrow and
suffering enough to disarm all hostility.

H.W. Longfellow

One ex-prisoner of war asked another, "Have you
forgiven your captors yet." The second one replied,
"No, NEVER!" "Then it seems like they still have you
in prison, don't they?' responded the first one.

Many of the world's major religions emphasize
forgiveness as one of their core attributes. Judaism
defines it as the cancellation of a debt so that the debtor

can be restored to right relationship with the offended individual(s). Christianity emphasizes a God who forgives those who turn to Him and encourages its followers to forgive as they have been forgiven. Islam believes in the ability of God to forgive all sins. While Buddhism is not a theistic religion, its doctrines of compassion and forbearance come close to the notion of forgiveness. Compassion has to do with the easing of suffering of all sentient beings. Look with mercy rather than judgment on the offender. Forbearance involves letting go of resentment toward the offending one.

While these views have been around thousands of years, only recently have psychologists turned their attention to forgiveness and its importance for both psychological and physical reasons. Toward the end of the 20th century, social scientists began studying forgiveness. In 1998, the philanthropist Sir John Templeton began a campaign to provide 10 million in funding for scientific research on forgiveness.

DEFINITIONS OF FORGIVENESS

Forgiveness occurs when an individual who has been hurt or offended gives up his or her desire to avoid the person who hurt him or her, or gives up the desire to exact revenge on the person. He or she seeks reconciliation between them if it is safe and possible.

It is important to distinguish forgiveness from pardoning (which is a legal concept), condoning (which includes justifying the offense), excusing (which implies that a transgression was committed because of extenuating circumstances), forgetting (which implies that the memory of a transgression has decayed or slipped out of conscious awareness); and denial (which implies an unwillingness or inability to perceive the harmful injuries that one has incurred). [1] These processes are often incorrectly substituted for forgiveness and lead to the confusion many have in understanding forgiveness.

In part because of the many confusing views of what it means, forgiveness is difficult for many in our culture. One common view is that forgiveness means glossing over the wrongs another causes us, whitewashing the hurts and pains others have caused us. Forgiveness then can become a kind of emotional dishonesty. For example, his older brother hits little Johnny. Mother steps in and orders the older brother to say he is sorry. She then asks Johnny to make up with the older brother before he has had an opportunity to process his feelings of anger, hurt, and vengeance. Mother short-circuits the process. In essence, she is telling Johnny to discount his feelings of hurt.

This pattern of childhood expresses itself in adults who believe that any negative behavior toward another can be remedied or made right with a superficial, glib, "Forgive me, I'm sorry." This glossed over view of forgiveness is what the martyred Lutheran pastor, Dietrich Bonhoeffer, called "cheap grace." Cheap grace does not demand anything from the offending party:

no remorse, no changed behavior. Marital therapist Janis Abrahams Spring calls this "cheap forgiveness." She defines it as "… a quick and easy pardon with no processing of emotion and no coming to terms with injury; it's compulsive, unconditional, and a unilateral attempt at peacemaking for which you ask nothing in return"(p. 15).

Another cultural view of forgiveness is that when one forgives, one should forget the offense. Live and let live is the attitude. Regarding the small hurts we inevitably cause each other simply because we are human, this is probably good advice. I have worked with persons who were "injustice collectors." Like the proverbial elephant that never forgets, these people offer litanies of the minor hurts, grievances, slights, and rude behavior they have experienced from others. For them, healing comes when they can release and let go of these minor resentments and forget them. When it comes to minor hurts, forgiveness and forgetting is good advice for our emotional and spiritual well-being.

However, when it comes to major hurts, forgiveness does not mean forgetting. Should a Holocaust survivor forget the cruel barbarism of the Nazis? Should a physically or emotionally abused wife or sexually abused child forget the violence inflicted on them? Should a mother whose teenage son or daughter is killed by a drunken driver forget? Usually this exhortation to forgive and forget comes from one who has never been deeply hurt by another.

THE DEVELOPMENT OF THE CAPACITY TO FORGIVE

The capacity for forgiveness grows with age. Young children are generally the least willing to forgive and older adults more willing. Why is this? Researchers have drawn on the theories of moral developmental expert Lawrence Kohlberg to explain this process. In his view of how moral development proceeds, Kohlberg reasons that in early stages of moral development, children forgive only when the offended one has obtained revenge or the transgressor has made restitution. In the middle stage, the person forgives because religious, social, or moral pressures evoke compliance. At the higher stages, people forgive because it promotes a harmonious society and is an expression of unconditional love.

The personality characteristics of the forgiving individual have also been studied. Forgiving people report less depression, anxiety and hostility than their non-forgiving counterparts. When people feel less chronic hostility, they tend to have fewer cardiovascular problems, fewer heart attacks, and less shame, agitation, and rumination. They do not get or stay as agitated. They are less narcissistic and exploitive and more empathic. Distilling these characteristics to its essence, the capacity to forgive has been found to relate strongly with the qualities of agreeableness and emotional stability.

THE PROCESS OF FORGIVENESS

Forgiveness is a process. It is an act of the heart; a movement to let go of the pain, resentment, and outrage that has been carried as a burden. It has many stages—grief, rage, sorrow, fear and confusion. Depending upon the nature of the injury and the relationship with the offender, you will experience many feelings in the process of forgiving.

Forgiveness is not primarily for others, but for us. Forgiveness is essential to our physical well-being. Psychosomatic medicine, which investigates and treats the effects of beliefs and emotions on the body, reminds us of this. Harbored resentments, grievances, hostilities can literally make us physically ill.

In his groundbreaking work on the ingredients that make persons prime candidates for heart disease and heart attacks, Dr. Redman Williams at Duke Medical Center identified hostility and cynicism as two prime ingredients. My clinical work supports that finding.

I have worked with people clinically who held onto resentments and grievances toward family members for so long that they became emotionally and physically ill. I was working at a large private hospital and was talking to an elderly man with serious health issues, heart disease and terminal cancer. He had just been moved from ICU to a regular room. I noticed that there were not any get-well cards or flowers displayed. As he told his story, a picture emerged of a man who through the years had alienated himself from family members by his anger, hostility, and other negative behavior. Now he was dying and feeling very alone and isolated. Through the course of my visits he began to trust me and shared some of his pain. We talked about the ways he hurt his children. We also discussed how he could die with some peace in his heart. I asked him if he were willing to participate in a forgiveness ritual. I had him picture in his mind as vividly as possible the family members he had hurt and then ask for their forgiveness. This was a very moving experience for us both. At the end of the experience, he said that a "huge weight had been lifted from his heart." He felt at peace. Not many days later he died.

Look what happens to us physically when we do not forgive. The body manufactures masses of "high voltage" chemicals like adrenaline, noradrenaline, hormone and cortisol. When too many of these high voltage chemicals hold up in the blood stream, a person becomes a prime candidate for some specific ills, such as a vascular tension headache. The heart begins to pound like a sledgehammer in the chest, the muscles in the neck and shoulders begin to constrict, and abdominal pains develop. If the situation continues, gastric ulcers, gastritis or irritable bowel syndrome can result. With forgiveness, on the other hand, the anger and resentment dissolve. The body stops pouring high-voltage chemicals into the bloodstream. The healing begins.

Forgiving is also important because it frees us of the role of victim. Rabbi Harold Kushner, author of

When Bad Things Happen to Good People, tells of a woman in his congregation who came to see him. She is a single mother, divorced, working to support her and three young children. "Since my husband walked out on us," she says," every month is a struggle to pay our bills. I have to tell my kids we have no money to go to the movies, while he is living it up with his new wife in another state. How can you tell me to forgive him?" Kushner answers, "I am not asking you to forgive him because what he did was acceptable. It wasn't; it was mean and selfish. I'm asking you to forgive him because he doesn't deserve the power to live in your head and turn you into a bitter, angry woman. I'd like to see him out of your life emotionally as completely as he is out of it physically, but you keep holding on to him. You are not hurting him by holding on to resenting him, but you are hurting yourself."

As this example makes clear, forgiveness is not condoning negative behavior, someone else's or your own. It is not pretending everything is just fine when it is not, or assuming an attitude of superiority or self-righteousness. Instead, it is a decision to see beyond the limits of another's personality, to be willing to accept responsibility for your own perceptions, to shift your perceptions repeatedly, and to gradually transform yourself from being a helpless victim of your circumstances to becoming a powerful loving creator of your world.

As mentioned, empathy has been found to be an important ingredient in forgiveness. Empathy refers to the ability to identify with another's experience while being clear that it is the other's experience. Empathy involves putting ourselves in the perspective of another. It is walking in another's moccasins for three miles.

Dr. Everett Worthington taught others how to forgive: one night he had to become his own best pupil. The call came on New Years Day, 1996. His brother Mike's voice was shaky. "I have some bad news," he said. "Mama has been murdered."

In the next five minutes, Mike sketched for him what he saw when he and his stepson, David, walked into the scene. That night, Worthington, his brother, and his sister talked about it. Their mother had been beaten to death with a crowbar. Her body was then assaulted with a wine bottle. Rage bubbled up in him like lava. He heard himself saying, "I'd like to have that murderer alone in a room with just a baseball bat. I'd beat his brains out!"

That night about 3:00 AM, he fought the bedcovers, imagining the scenes of violence, his thoughts overflowing with hatred and revenge. Ironically, only days before he had finished co writing a book, *To Forgive Is Human: How To Put Your Past In The Past*. Finally, his own book brought him up short. Did he really believe, as they had written, that empathy was a key to forgiving? Could he empathize with the person who had murdered his mother? Or was that book just for other people?

He did not know who did it and never would find out. But that night he tried to picture the crime scene. He imagined how a pair of youths might feel as they stood in the dark street preparing to rob the house. Perhaps they had been caught at robbery previously. They would have been keyed up. The house was dark; no car was in the driveway. "No one's home," they must have thought. Perhaps one said, "They're at a New Years Eve party." They did not know that Worthington's mother did not drive.

A quick rap of the crowbar and they were in, hastily emptying drawers, dumping the contents on the floor. Worthington imagined their shock when her voice came from behind. "What are you doing in here?" "Oh, no!" one must have thought, "I'll go to jail. She is ruining my life." He lashed out with his crowbar, slamming his mother three times. Panicked, the youths went crazy, trashing the house, both for having their plans ruined, and for the shame of having murdered.

Worthington felt he understood better what had happened. He writes, "Whoever murdered my mom did a terrible thing. Nothing will change that. Through empathy, however, I saw that he had lashed out in fear, panic, guilt, and anger. I thought of how I had talked about beating him to death with a baseball bat. I was willing to do what he did, only with more forethought, more naked malice." [2]

He thought, "Whose heart is darker?" He almost spoke aloud. When he thought about the evil that he was capable of plotting, he was humbled. He saw his own guilt over planning revenge. He writes, "As a Christian, I believed that even as I confessed my evil intent, I would receive divine forgiveness for it. I felt that forgiveness flood me. I knew what the youth needed. So I forgave him, and I have since felt peace."

EXERCISE

1. Where are you on the path toward peace and healing? Forgiveness is a healing journey for both your body and soul. Yet, even if you know in your heart that you want or need to forgive someone, the path toward peace can be difficult. To move forward, it often helps to have an accurate sense of where you are right now. The following check-up was developed from a longer test created by Susan Wade Brown, Ph.D., as part of her doctoral dissertation in psychology at Fuller Theological Seminary, in Pasadena, CA., edited by Robert Enright, Ph.D., and professor of psychology at the University of Washington. Experts including Dr. Everett Worthington, creator of the REACH program for forgiveness, have used the full test, designed with therapists in mind, in many scientific studies.

Take about five minutes to assess your thoughts, feelings and behaviors related to forgiveness. You may find, as many others have, that simply taking this check-up moves you forward toward peace. Think about the specific person you want to measure your forgiveness toward. Rate each item to the extent that the thoughts, feelings, and behaviors match your own.

0 = Strongly disagree/**1** = Disagree/**2** = Neutral/

3 = Agree/**4** = Strongly agree

1. I'm going to get even.

Strongly disagree   0   1   2   3   4 Strongly agree

2. I'll make them pay.

Strongly disagree   0   1   2   3   4 Strongly agree

3. I replay the offense in my mind, dwelling on it.

Strongly disagree   0   1   2   3   4 Strongly agree

4. I think about them with anger.

Strongly disagree   0   1   2   3   4 Strongly agree

5. I can understand where they are coming from.

Strongly disagree   0   1   2   3   4 Strongly agree

6. I have a clear ability to see their good points.

Strongly disagree   0   1   2   3   4 Strongly agree

7. I prayed for them, asking God to bless them.

Strongly disagree   0   1   2   3   4 Strongly agree

8. I told God I forgive them.

Strongly disagree   0   1   2   3   4 Strongly agree

9. My resentment is gone.

Strongly disagree   0   1   2   3   4 Strongly agree

10. I feel peace.

Strongly disagree   0   1   2   3   4 Strongly agree

11. I keep as much distance between us as possible.

Strongly disagree   0   1   2   3   4 Strongly agree

12. I live as if they don't exist, or never existed.

Strongly disagree   0   1   2   3   4 Strongly agree

13. I looked for the source of the problem and tried to correct it.

Strongly disagree   0   1   2   3   4 Strongly agree

14. I took steps toward reconciliation: wrote them, called them, showed concern.

Strongly disagree   0   1   2   3   4 Strongly agree

7
SPIRITUALITY

If a man has a 'why' to live, he can bear with almost any how.

Frederick Nietzsche

Many of us remember John Tesh as one of the co-anchors of the popular show *Entertainment Tonight*. Billed as the "most widely watched entertainment show in the world," Tesh and co-anchor Mary Hart five nights a week gave viewers the latest news and gossip on celebrities. In an interview, he later recalled that he was richly rewarded for hosting the show, but something was missing in his life. The fame and fortune did not fill his inner emptiness and he was searching for something more. That growing and gnawing emptiness led him to leave the program and continue the search. Like many of his contemporaries, he had been an active churchgoer. Reaching adulthood, he left the church. Later, he found a faith community where his questions and doubts were honored and accepted. He felt that he had come "home."

This search for something more is universal. Psychologist William James described it as the inner movement of the divine. Spirituality is our search for the sacred, the something more.

Spirituality is one of the emphases of positive psychology. In its elaboration of the three pillars of a positive psychology—positive emotions, positive character and positive institutions—there is a recognition that spirituality contributes to living the good and authentic life.

It is important to note that until the end of the twentieth century, psychologists paid little attention to religion and spirituality except in very negative terms. Oh, there were a few voices crying in the wilderness (i.e., C.G. Jung, William James) but their messages like the prophets of old were ignored and dismissed by mainstream psychology. Psychology of religion scholar Kenneth Pargament has suggested that "…. psychologists have tended to: (a) ignore spirituality, (b) view spirituality as pathological, and (c) view spirituality as a process that can be reduced to more basic underlying psychological, social and physiological functions." [3]

However, toward the end of the century, psychology has taken a more balanced and serious look at the importance of spirituality in human functioning. Some factors that have contributed to this turnaround are the "graying of the baby-boomers." Many boomers are finding that the sleekest SUV, the Rolex watch, the newest and more features-laden laptop do not bring them happiness in the long term. Like Peggy Lee, they ask, "Is this all there is?". Many seem to be looking for something more. Another factor spurring interest in spirituality is the growing body of research suggesting the relevance of spirituality for human functioning—mental health, parenting and mental functioning, the outcomes of stressful life experience. Spirituality cannot be ignored.

Any discussion of spirituality must include consideration of its relationship to religion, inevitably, the two are confused. Religion represents the ways in which the experience of the sacred becomes organized, embodied and institutionalized. From earliest times, individuals have sought concrete ways to honor and express the experience of the divine whether in ritual, song, story, or worship. Part of the power of institutional religions is that they provide definite pronouncements about what ultimately matters. The believers then surrender (devote their lives to) the authority of the institution and its tradition. Institutional religions typically focus their followers on some sacred event in the past in which God's way was revealed. This revelation then becomes an institutionalized pattern to which devotees compare their own experience. If their experience conforms to the pattern, they can interpret it as good.

By contrast, in spirituality, there is an attempt to find God in the personal experience of the spiritual seeker rather through the authority of a previous event. Spirituality is one's relationship to the transcendent, the sacred, and the power beyond oneself. Whether one calls that 'beyond ness' God, a Higher Power, Cosmic Consciousness or the Divine Within is not nearly as important as the recognition that one's life is part of a greater life energy in which all living things participate. Just as a drop of seawater encompasses the ocean but does not completely contain it, so one's life can express a glimmer of the divine but not exhaust it. Professor Jared Kass, Ph.D. once asked a woman to define her spirituality. She described her spirituality this way; "Listening to my inner self is like drawing water from a well that reaches down into an underground sea. It is part of me, yet it is greater than me."

Spirituality is derived from the Latin word *spiritus*, which means the breath of life. In the Old Testament, the Hebrew word for breath is the same word used for the spirit of God. which, as the Russian philosopher Berdyaev (1939) noted, has been used as a synonym for wisdom, intelligence, the capacity to reason, and the soul or any nonphysical life.

Religion and spirituality can either enhance well-being and communal life or destroy it. More people have been killed in religious wars than all other wars combined. In other words, spirituality is not inherently good. Jim Jones and Jonestown, the Crusade, the Spanish Inquisition, the Salem Witch Hunts, the German state church's affiliation with Hitler are vivid and painful reminders of the demonization of the sacred. Religion and spirituality can be "hazardous to your health."

POSITIVE PSYCHOLOGY AND RELIGION/SPIRITUALITY

Positive Psychology has aimed its spotlight on spirituality for a number of reasons. Perhaps the most important one is the conviction that from an authentic spirituality comes the virtues that are essential to living the good life—the capacity for love, justice, intimacy, compassion, goodness and optimism. "By their fruits ye shall know them" (Matt. 7:16). These virtues are believed to be essential to well-lived life and the foundations of society. If a person does not walk his talk, his spirituality is superficial.

Religion is not just concerned about saving the souls of individuals but whether they have soles on their shoes.

Researchers have found that churches that promote a sense of social responsibility and justice do much good in their communities. These churches take seriously the second commandment to love the neighbor. One important test of a church is what it does for the underdog: the underprivileged, the marginalized sectors of society. Asking the question, " Am I my brother's keeper? is as old as the Genesis story and as current as the family on welfare, the young man with AIDS, and the young girl with a cancerous brain tumor. Examples of faith-based groups taking seriously the second commandment to love the neighbor are not hard to find. The Council for Urban Peace and Justice, a coalition of faith-based national organizations, recently gathered gang leaders from 30 cities to explore a redirection toward nonviolence and the healing of the streets. Folks in Pittsburgh, PA created the City Pride Bakery, " a worker owned consortium of unemployed, unemployable, welfare homeless and others who joined forces to make a new life." The newspaper account indicated that this project was supported by 25 private and public organizations, 3 religious orders, and 4 banks! Many African American churches promote the well-being of their communities by providing a wide range of services such as counseling, financial support, housing and clothing to those in need. It is not surprising that African American churches in the late '50's and '60's were one of the major forces behind the civil rights movement.

SPIRITUALITY AND HEALTH

Most of the major western spiritual traditions recognize that the human being is a mind-body-spirit organism. The Apostle Paul writes that the body is the temple of the soul. The Judeo-Christian commandment to love God with all one heart, mind, soul and strength. In one of the healings he performed, Jesus declared: "Thy faith has made thee whole." (Mark 5:34)

Spirituality and medicine have been intertwined from earliest times. The earliest physicians were religious figures in tribes: the priests, shamans, and the medicine men and women. Cardiologist Bruce Cortis points out that disease originally was considered to be supernatural and those who dealt with diseases were ones considered to have power over the spirit. In the sixteenth century, surgeon Ambrose noted in one surgical report, "I dressed the wound and God healed it." In the seventeenth century, in his "Discourse on Method," French philosopher and mathematician Rene Descartes stated his philosophy, "I think, therefore I am". This marked the beginning of a reductionistic viewpoint that valued truth only in objective ways. It did not consider the unseen forces and influences that impacted health and disease. The upshot was that in order to be more scientific, medicine cut its moorings away from a faith belief structure. While there were a few physicians who used a patient's spiritual resources in treatment, the majority of health care professionals viewed healing a nontheistic, materialistic way.

In the latter part of the twentieth century, a few pioneers began to write and publish on the healing power of faith. In 1976, neuropsychologist Robert Adler at the University of Rochester demonstrated that the immune system, once believed not to be influenced by one's thoughts or emotions can be changed. His work demonstrated the importance of belief on emotional and physical functioning. This work sparked interest in the role of faith, belief, expectation, and the placebo effect on health. A cardiologist at Harvard, Herbert Benson, demonstrated how teaching patients the relaxation response could lower blood pressure, racing thoughts and insomnia. Later in his laboratory he investigated how patients using sacred words from their faith tradition could achieve even better results than the relaxation response. In his book *Timeless Healing,* Benson makes a case for the notion that our brains are "wired for faith." Another pioneer in the interface of medicine and spirituality is physician and author Larry Dossey, an articulate spokesman for complementary medicine. His areas of research have focused on investigating the effects of prayer (positive and harmful effects) and what he calls non-local healing. That is, do my prayers in Bradenton, FL for healing someone in Seattle, WA do any good? Do they make a difference? His book *Healing Words* was a study of the few solid studies on prayer and was a best-seller on the New York Times list for a number of weeks.

Religious involvement has been highlighted as one important and positive link to psychological and physical well being. Religious involvement is defined as weekly church or synagogue attendance, prayer and reading of sacred writings. Dr. Harold Koening and colleagues at Duke University Medical Center studied the coping and recovery rate of depressed elderly male patients. His research demonstrated that patients who were regular church attendees make a quicker recovery from the effects of depression than those who were given only antidepressant medication.

Prayer has been found to play a significant role in coping and promoting well being. In his book *Psychology And The Religion Of Coping* Kenneth Pargament found that patients who were able to surrender their situation to God fared better on a number of psychological measures than those who tried to bargain or those who remained angry. He also identified how differences in a person's religious spiritual solving style can affect the ability to cope with adversity. Four styles were identified:

1. A self-directing style. Individuals with this style are calling the shots. They may believe in a higher power; however, they mainly rely on themselves to solve problems.

2. A deferring style. Individuals with this style are more passive. I am not able to handle the situation. I must turn it over to God.

3. A collaborative style. Individuals with this style see themselves working with God to deal with the problem at hand. An old prayer begins with the words, "Help me to know, Lord, that nothing is going to happen today that we both can't handle."

4. A surrendering style. Individuals make a conscious decision to surrender aspects of the situation that are truly beyond their control. The

famous AA prayer begins with the words"…help me to accept the things that I cannot change."

Each of these styles of prayer has an important place in the individual's life. Each style seems to be adaptive in a wide range of situations. Individuals tend to feel empowered (with God on their side) and do what they can to improve the situation. The self-directive style is effective, largely because people tend to fare better when they perceive a situation as controllable. The exception to this is when the situation is largely uncontrollable. In extreme situations like the death of a family member, the surrendering to God is often the most effective. When nothing can be done to prevent the event, surrendering control provides an overwhelmed person with inner peace.

SPIRITUALITY AND THE SEARCH FOR MEANING

A world without God would be a flat, monochromatic world, a world without color or texture, and a world in which all days would be the same. Marriage would be a matter of biology, not fidelity. Old age would be seen as a time of weakness, not of wisdom. In a world like that, we would cast about desperately for any sort of diversion, for any distraction from the emptiness of our lives, because we would never have learned the magic of making some days and some hours special. (Kushner)

Part of living our strengths is connecting oneself to an overarching framework of meaning. Man is the only living creature who becomes anxious about the future, agonizes about his suffering and worries about his dying. We seek some meaning to it all. Transcendent realities can prove to be very important. They are like the North Star that guides the traveler through the darkness. If we are lost in the forest, we seek a way out. Admittedly, science does offer us an understanding of our observable, physical world, but how do we grasp the meaning of our lives? Global meanings concern the large questions, *What is the meaning of life? What is the meaning of it all?* And more personally, *What does my life mean?*

At the end of our lives, most of us probably would hope that our lives mattered to our loved ones and friends, that our little acts of kindness, care, compassion, and generosity would live on in those whose lives we touched; and that we make some small difference for love and justice in our corner of the world. Living our spirituality is one important way to make this happen.

I want to close this chapter with a poem by Denise Levertov. She expresses in these words our hope that the heart of the mystery in which we live is gracious.

As swimmers dare

to lie fact to sky

and water bears them,

as hawks rest upon air

and air sustains them,

so would I learn to attain

freefall, and float

into Creator Spirit's deep embrace,

knowing no effort earns

that all surrounding grace.

EXERCISES

1. Create a time line of your life. List those marker events and stepping stones that impacted your life, positively and negatively. Review the events for their contribution to your own sense of the sacred. The sacred addresses us through ordinary events. The stuff of our life is always speaking to us.

2. Take out your checkbook register. Look over the last six months entries. After eliminating the monthly fixed expenses (i.e., housing, food, utilities, insurance, gas) see what these purchases include. Money is symbolic. It tells us about what we value and prize. What does your spending tell you about your values? What

do you prize? Whatever is of ultimate value to you is your God.

3. Make up a menu for the rest of your life, considering: What do I have an appetite for? What do I want to taste again and again or, for the first time? What do I not want to stomach any longer? What, for me, would be a healthy diet for living? Do not censor your wants nor try to make them politically or theologically correct.

8
RESILIENCE

"You're riding high in April, shot down in May.
That's Life"

> Words & Music by Dean Kay and Kelly
>
> Gordon

There stood Beethoven, gravely ill and totally deaf. Eyes closed, he kept conducting the orchestra after they had ceased their performance and the audience had risen to its feet in thunderous applause. As a singer stepped from the choir to turn him around to see those whose shouts of "Bravo" resonated through the concert hall, tears of elation filled his eyes. Perhaps the worst loss a composer could experience had been the catalyst for a remarkable adaptive creativity that allowed him to transcend his tortures to become immersed in the thrill of conducting the premiere of his Ninth Symphony, the "Ode to Joy." At that moment, and not only in spite or but because of his adversity, Beethoven had experienced the thrill of thriving through adversity. [1]Beethoven demonstrated the ability to be resilient.

Resilience is the ability to bounce back from adversity. It is one of the character strengths that positive psychology is investigating. *Webster's Dictionary* defines resilience as an act of springing back, rebounding; the capacity of a strained body to recover. It is not surprising that positive psychology is looking at this capacity because it focuses of human strengths and virtues rather than weaknesses and pathology.

In a very thought-provoking article in the *American Psychologist*, Dr. George Bonanno asks the question, have we underestimated the human capacity to thrive after extremely aversive events? He makes an important distinction between the concepts of resilience and recovery. He notes that *recovery* is best understood as a process in which normal functioning temporarily gives way to threshold or sub threshold psychopathology (e.g., symptoms of depression or posttraumatic stress disorder-PTSD), usually for a period of at least several months, and then gradually returns to pre-event levels. By contrast, *resilience* reflects the ability to maintain a stable equilibrium. He states that resilience to loss and trauma pertains to the ability of adults in otherwise normal circumstances, who are exposed to an isolated and potentially highly disruptive event, such as the death of a close relation or a violent or life-threatening situation, to maintain relatively stable, healthy levels of psychological and physical functioning." [2]

This distinction is important because it is a reminder that resilience is strength and not simply the absence of pathology. Resilient individuals may experience temporary disturbances in normal functioning (e.g., several weeks of sporadic preoccupation or restless sleep) but generally keep on going in productive ways.

Studies have shown that many people in the direst situations have demonstrated the capacity to become resilient. These studies have included children raised in families with parents with mental illness or substance abuse problems. Two researchers in a longitudinal study interviewed children at risk in Hawaii, and followed them for forty years. When asked about their strengths, these individuals focused on similar assets: compassion and caring, ability to get along with others, sense of optimism, capacity to plan and solve problems, creativity and hard work. Many of these individuals came to view the adversities in their lives as important living experiences that served as challenges to overcome rather than as great tragedies or mistakes from which to suffer.

The bottom line is that we have within us the capacity to become resilient; to develop what psychologists Brooks and Goldstein call a "resilient mindset" and what Paul Pearsall calls "The Beethoven Factor." In its research on resilience, positive psychology touts the fact that the potential for individuals to handle adversity may be far greater than previously recognized.

DEVELOPING RESILIENCE

Each of us can learn to interpret and respond to events in ways that reinforce hope and resilience rather than despair. I am not suggesting that people beset by pessimism and helplessness lack the fortitude to better their condition or outlook on life but rather that many do not appreciate the power they possess to alter self-defeating perceptions that they have. These negative tapes, whether in the form of blaming others, God or life for their difficulties locks them in a victim mentality. Such a mindset does not change the situation but only mires them down even more in the quicksand of self-pity, depression and despair. As a therapist I have witnessed the transformations that occur when individuals refuse to be a victim and exercise what control they can in their lives. One of my patients, a young mother, when she learned that she had an inoperable form of cancer, moved forward with her life, putting her affairs in order, moving in with family members and setting out to enjoy her remaining time with her daughter, her family and her friends.

Adversity comes to each of us, whether in the form of a major illness, job loss, poverty, death of a loved one, divorce or natural or man-caused trauma. As the Buddha reminds us, life is a mixture of 10,000 joys and 10,000 sorrows.

How can we become resilient? Is it just for a select few? Ralph Waldo Emerson notes that this characteristic is universal. "The hero is no braver than an ordinary man, but he is brave five minutes longer."

First, resilience can be developed through what University of Chicago researchers call *hardiness.* They studied middle and senior level managers who were let go during a major downsizing at a large company in Illinois. They were interested in discovering the differences between those who effectively coped with the situation and those who did not. According to the researchers, the resilient individuals exhibited the "three c's." They exercised what *control* they could; saw the situation as a *challenge* rather than a defeat; and were *committed* to something or someone bigger than themselves (i.e., family, God, a higher power).

Psychologist Paul Pearsall describes working with a patient who was diagnosed with leukemia. He asked her for a time in her life where she or someone close to her seemed to have experienced the "three c's of hardiness." After thinking for a while, she said, "I guess the closest I can come to being hardy when my husband cheated on me and left me and the kids. I was devastated, but something in me kept me going. I guess I did it for the kids. I was really committed to remaining a good parent for them. After feeling depressed, I sort of got pissed off and took what happened to me as a challenge to be a great parent and have a good life despite what happened. I remember feeling getting back in control again. It wasn't easy, but we made it." [3]

This example reminds us that hardiness is no guarantee of freedom from suffering. Do you remember the story of Job in the Old Testament? Job was living a healthy, prosperous, bountiful life, when suddenly, everything changed. He went from being on top of the world to suffering from a painful, disfiguring disease. His wealth evaporated and, worst of all, he lost his seven sons. Through it all, however, his enduring patience and unshakable faith carried him through. Nothing that happened to him changed how hardy he was or how he thought about the meaning of life. If we knew more about his life before all these calamities befell him, we might discover other instances of Job's resilient spirit and the manner in which he coped with challenges in his life. The resilient spirit is like a muscle; the more it is exercised, the stronger it becomes. I have worked with people who when facing challenges would draw upon their memories of other times when they dealt with a challenge effectively.

When I think of resilient people I think of the psychiatrist Dr. Viktor Frankl. He was a survivor of a concentration camp in Nazi Germany. His wife, parents and all of his relatives, except his sister Stella, died in the camp. He wrote a book on those experiences, *Man's Search For Meaning,* which became an international bestseller. I first read the book when I was going through a very difficult time in my own life. Its inspiring message of hope and meaning gave me new resolve to get through the situation. My old tattered copy of the book is full of underlinings that I often go back to for inspiration. A particular meaningful underlining is as follows:

"We who live in concentration camps can remember the men who walked through the huts comforting others, giving away their last piece of bread. They may have been few in number, but they offer sufficient proof that everything can be taken away from a man but one thing: the last of the human freedoms-to choose one's attitude in any given set of circumstances, to choose one's own way." [5]

Our attitude in the face of adversity is a key element in getting through it. Nelson Mandela discovered the same truth as Frankl. He was locked up for twenty-seven years. At a certain point, he realized that, "My enemies could take it all, everything, but my mind and heart. I decided not to give them away." This insight helped him reestablish dignity and personal integrity. In spite of his suffering, Mandela continued to be a beacon for those who cherish freedom and justice. From 1994 until 1999, he served as the first democratically elected State President of South Africa. Though retired from public life, he lives quietly in his birthplace of Qunu, Transkei, and his writings and speeches continue to offer hope to so many in the world. His life is an example of the power of resilience to overcome great odds.

It is not only world leaders who offer models of resilience. Another excellent example was the popular actor, Christopher Reeve. For many he personified resilience. Many of us know his story. A gifted actor, he achieved stardom portraying Superman in several movies. On a beautiful spring afternoon in May 1995, his life changed suddenly. While participating in an equestrian event in the green fields outside Culpepper, Virginia, he was thrown off his horse and smashed into the ground. His injuries were so severe that he stopped breathing for more than three minutes. The impact was so stunning that his head had to be reattached to his spinal column. The result was paralysis from his neck down. Within seconds he went from being a virile and healthy young man to a quadriplegic, requiring a ventilator to take even a simple breath.

During one interview he candidly revealed that immediately following his accident he questioned whether it would be better if he just died. In subsequent years, while still experiencing at times an understandable sadness, he adapted a mind set filled with hope, a mind set that permitted him to continue to act in and direct movies, to give speeches and to become a very visible advocate for increased funding for research into spinal cord injuries. After several years, he astounded many by achieving some hand movement as well as sensation over much of his body. He became capable of breathing for up to 90 minutes without the aid of a ventilator. All of these are remarkable given the extent of his injuries.

Reeve wrote: "After you survive a traumatic event, the challenge is to make sense of it and to find a new and perhaps different way of living a meaningful life. I believe one of the key indicators of emotional health is the ability to function well in the present and make plans for the future. I'm able to do that. I can choose to stop thinking, 'I could have been sailing on this day five years ago,' and start thinking, 'What am I going to do today."[6] On October 10, 2004, Christopher Reeve passed away. He was only 52 years old and the world mourned his death. He brought hope and optimism to those suffering from spinal cord injuries and other central nervous system diseases. Most importantly, he taught us the power of resilience and showed us that each of us has an opportunity to live with that kind of courage and grace. Before he died, he said, "What I do is based on powers we all have inside us: the ability to endure, the ability to love, to carry on, to make the most of what we have—and you don't have to be a 'Superman' to do it."

When Hurricane Katrina battered the Gulf Coast, incredible stories surfaced about men and women braving the storm and helping neighbors and strangers to safety. One such remarkable person is trauma surgeon, Dr. Norman McSwain, Trauma Director at Charity Hospital and a professor at Tulane School of Medicine. As water continued to pour through the broken levees of New Orleans, muddy, polluted water was rising, trapping hundreds of patients and more than a thousand staff members at Tulane and Charity Hospital.

As generators failed and food ran low, McSwain rallied staff and patients wading through the treacherous floodwaters between hospitals to attend to patients. When helicopters arrived, he helped coordinate the amphibious evacuation. His resilient spirit is summed up in the words, "As a trauma surgeon, you never think things are hopeless. Maybe other people did. But my thought was always, " How am I going to solve this?" In these few words, Dr. McSwain describes a key attribute of resilience, which is: I will do what I can to change the situation or my attitude toward it.

In order to develop resilience, we need to create and maintain vibrant connections in our life and display compassion. It is difficult to be resilient if we do not nurture connections in our lives—connections to other people, to ideals, to our faith, to causes.

A table is only as strong as its legs and it is these relationships that form the foundation—the legs of our courage and resilience. Some adults truly enrich the lives of children, and are people from whom children gather strength. Even as adults we need people in our lives from which we gather strength.

Trisha Meili, the Central Park Jogger, who was savagely beaten, raped and left for dead, but recovered, took pride in always being the strong one but quickly saw after her attack that she could not make it without the help of others. She was willing to accept help. In her book, she says, "I held on to all the outstretched hands, feeling gratitude." It is simply not true that effective copers are rugged individualists. Often people who cope with trauma and tragedy are those who readily reach out for support when they need it. Today Trisha gives back what she was given. Her motivational speeches to medical and mental health groups and to those recovering from traumatic changes allow her to offer an outstretched hand to others in need of support and comfort.

Resilience is not only strengthened within us when we reach out for help but when we give help to others. It is true that when we genuinely give of ourselves to another we often receive more than we give. When we love someone, we often discover that rather than being emptied, we are filled. We find that love is inexhaustible. When we help someone—perhaps offering a listening ear, meeting a particular need or just being a friend— we often experience a tremendous 'high,' the personal satisfaction that we were there for that other person. These experiences make us feel good as a person. They take us out of ourselves.

After September 11, 2001, and the devastation of the terrorist attacks, I had the privilege of working with one of the survivors of that horrific event.   Dan was in one of the twin towers, attending a training program for new brokers. He recalls, "I was on a coffee break. I heard an explosion." He looked out the cracked windows and saw a blizzard of paper. When the plane hit the tower, he went down the stairwell and aided others to safety. When he came back to Sarasota, he felt strongly he had to do something to help. Dan and fellow survivors spent their time talking to over 100 church and community groups. It was healing for him and the people he spoke to, he stated later. The first series of talks raised $32,000 for the Fire Fighters of New York City. The following year, he organized an event, "Triumph over Tragedy," September 11, 2002. The event raised $100, 000 and the money was used locally by the Fire Department to buy ten Jaws of Life for the local fire fighters. Why did Dan do this? He wanted to help. He commented, "You see all those good people who didn't make it. Hard to believe. You owe something to them." He used this horrific experience to help others. This is a high use of resilience.

A resilient spirit not only reaches out to others, but commits itself to something greater than itself. An important ingredient of a resilient mindset is a meaning or purpose, which steadies us when life tumbles in. "You are riding high in April, shot down in May."

Sol Levenson is a muralist who demonstrates this resilient spirit. At 95, he is still going strong painting murals about the Shaker sect, Native Americans and

New England county fairs. His current project is a three-panel portrait of the Civil War at the Dartmouth Hitchcock Hospital in Lebanon, N.H.. He has won two Fulbright scholarships to study abroad. He does all his murals—for which he charges only the cost of materials—in the oncology section because his first wife died of cancer. Levenson comments, "The patients' conversations feed me."

A patient who was particularly inspired by Levenson was Janice Munro, a former nurse who had bilateral breast cancer. When she arrived for her first radiation session a few years ago, she spotted Levenson in the corner, painting. "There was so much energy and life in those murals, and that's what I wanted back in my life," she recalls. "When I looked at his murals, I forgot about the cancer and felt healthy. He lives life to the fullest every single day, and I realized that's what I had to do too.

In Viktor Frankl's experience in the concentration camp, a time of unspeakable horrors and degradation, the thing that kept him going was his search for a personal meaning to it all. He would spend time, composing in his mind chapters of a book that later became *Man's Search For Meaning*. He developed a new psychotherapy: logotherapy. Translated, it means a therapy of meaning.

In contrast to Freud who believed man is primarily motivated by pleasure and seeks to avoid suffering, Frankl believed man is primarily motivated to seek meaning. Of all the mammals, man is the only one who asks why. Nietzsche's question, "He who has a why to live can bear with almost any how," became Frankl's question in the concentration camp. This question is a spiritual one because it asks about ultimate concerns, what really matters. What is my life about? What is the center I can go to when everything around me is in chaos? Where do I find the power to see it through? For many, the answer to those questions is found in spirituality. Spirituality is our relationship to the something more, whether we call that God, higher power, or anything else. If you peel away much of the dogma, doctrine and theology of the major spiritual traditions, you are left with a powerful assertion: We matter to God. We are not alone in this incredible, often puzzling and difficult world: incomprehensible at times, the place where we experience much joy and deep sorrow.

Spirituality is an important ingredient of resilience. It can be an effective anchor in helping us deal with challenge. In Trisha Meili's experience, she came to believe that there is a higher power of some sort and felt that she saw God's grace in all the people who reached out to her. Successful copers often develop a new mission. They are glad they are still here, but ask themselves what are they going to do now? As I think about resilience, I am reminded of what playwright Samuel Beckett wrote: "Ever tried. Ever Failed. No matter. Try again. Fail again. Fail better."

We tend to underestimate our own resilience. Striving and overcoming obstacles can bring joy and focus to life.

SUGGESTED EXERCISES

1. Who are the two or three people who serve as charismatic adults in my life? What have they done that has prompted me to list them in this way?

2. Who are the people who would say that I am the charismatic adult in their life and why?

3. Aside from relationships with people, what other activities in my life supply me with a sense of connectedness?

9
KINDNESS

Let us be kind to one another, for most of us are fighting hard battles.

Scottish preacher Ian McAllen

Of the character strengths and virtues discussed so far, kindness has one of the greater effects on raising our level of happiness. It is an important ingredient of the good life. This is paradoxical because, as we shall see, kindness expressed to another without strings or conditions (i.e., less ego-involvement) is the most potent. The great humanitarian Albert Schweitzer comments, "I don't know what your destiny will be, but one thing

I do know: the only ones among you who will be really happy are those who have sought and found how to serve." This sentiment is echoed by physicist and Nobel Prize winner Albert Einstein who said, "Many times a day I realize how much my own outer and inner life is built upon the labors of my fellow man, both living and dead, and how earnestly I must exert myself in order to give in return as much as I have received."

What is kindness? Kindness is both a state of mind and a set of behaviors. As a state of mind it means: 1) a quality of being warm-hearted and considerate and human and sympathetic; 2) a tendency to be kind and forgiving; and 3) a kind act. There are a number of closely related behaviors that are included under the umbrella of kindness: generosity, nurturance, care, compassion, and altruistic love. All of these have in common *an orientation of the self toward the other as worthy of regard and attention for no utilitarian reason but for their own sake.* This definition of kindness needs to be distinguished from behaviors of "kindness" that are reciprocal or calculated.

People who rate high with kindness as one of their highest character strengths (see chapter 2) would strongly endorse statements such as the following:

+ Others are important to me.

+ Giving is more important than receiving.

+ I am not the center of the universe but part of a common humanity.

+ People who are suffering need compassion.

+ It is important to help everyone, not just family and friends.

The major spiritual traditions regard kindness as one of the highest virtues. In Judaism, kindness is called *chesed*, which implies the giving of oneself to another without regard to compensation. The rabbis of the Talmud considered kindness to be one of the three distinguishing marks of the Jew. Christianity directs its followers to be "kind to one another as God is kind toward you." Such kindness is part of agape love, which is unlimited, unconditional, and accepting. There is a marvelous story of a man who stood before God, his heart breaking from the pain and injustice of the world. Why don't you send help?" God responded, "I did send help. I sent you."

One of the inevitable questions raised in a discussion of kindness is this, why are we kind to another? Is it simply an egotistical act or is it altruistic? Philosophers and psychologists are divided on this issue. One tradition, "universal egoism," suggests that every "kind" act is ultimately done to benefit the self. The other tradition, "altruism," believes that people are, in fact, able to act with the ultimate goal of benefiting someone else.

Ben Dean, Ph.D. defines the case simply and precisely. The case against altruism basically has three reasons. Altruism offers these "selfish benefits." [1]

THE CASE AGAINST ALTRUISM

1. Doing something kind reduces the tension created by our experience of empathy and inaction. It can be physically and psychologically uncomfortable to see someone in need of support (e.g., a homeless person shivering during winter, a friend who lost a parent, a child being verbally abused by a parent). Helping relieves this tension.

2. A kind act allows us to avoid social sanction or personal guilt for failing to help. The disapproval of friends and family members and coworkers often is strong sanction for not helping. Selfish, insensitive, heartless, mean---these are labels we wish to avoid.

3. Kindness confers social and personal rewards. When we do the "right " thing, we earn the approval of others and feel good about ourselves. A theory of "reciprocal altruism" suggests

that kind acts are most often directed toward individuals who are likely to repay us in the future. If you offer to cut the grass of your neighbor when they are on vacation, then they will likely do the same for you. Evolutionary psychologist Geoffrey Miller noted that a truly anonymous act of kindness is the exception. For example, most "anonymous" donations are no secret to the giver's immediate family. Miller does not deny that most people have pure intentions when they donate money or time; but he does question why feelings of empathy and a proclivity to help evolved in the first place. He suggests that they evolved because acting with kindness and generosity confers social rewards.

THE CASE FOR ALTRUSIM

Dean notes that since the 1980's around 25 experiments have tested whether these selfish benefits are enough to explain altruistic behavior. Consider, for example, self-benefit #1: Doing something kind reduces the tension created by our experience of empathy and inaction. In experiments, individuals are placed in situations where they are likely to feel empathy toward someone in need (the tension mounts) and then experiments vary how easy it is for them to escape from that situation. If individuals were primarily motivated by a desire to reduce tension, then they would choose to escape from this situation when this was easy (e.g., nobody would know that they decided not to help). If, on the other hand, individuals were motivated by the desire to alleviate the distress of someone in trouble, then an easy escape would do nothing to relieve this tension. Results consistently support the second explanation.

There have been other experiments designed to pit a "helping others" motivation against more selfish ones (e.g., avoiding social sanctions, avoiding guilt, obtaining social or personal rewards). The results lend support to the other-oriented motivation.

THE DEVELOPMENT OF KINDNESS

How is kindness developed? Some researchers believe that kindness originally developed from the time when people lived in small groups of hunters and gatherers. They depended highly on each other not only for food and shelter but also for survival. New York psychologist Linda R. Caporall cites a series of studies conducted over ten years, which demonstrated that human nature is basically social, not selfish and she agrees that altruism probably stems back to hunter/gatherer times.

Adult's propensity for kindness and prosocial behavior can probably be predicted on the basis of their behavior during childhood and adolescence. Young adults' self-reported prosocial dispositions are related to the degree of empathy, sympathy and prosocial behavior they manifested years earlier. In an article in the *Noetic Sciences Review,* researcher Christi Kiefer found that the altruists she studied "came from families that were warm and nurturing. The emotional self-acceptance they developed in that environment liberated them to be generative, creative, playful, and relaxed." Also they learned a sense of social responsibility from their parents or from another significant person in their early lives—a sense that "committed them to action on behalf of others in their community." [3] Certain personality traits of altruistic people have been studied that enable them to reach out to others. Samuel P. Oliner and Pearl M. Oliner studied the "rescuers" who provided help to the Jews during Hitler's reign of terror. These people were altruistic—so much so they often risked their own lives and safety. Oliner believes that altruism is fueled by "empathy, allegiance to their group or institutional norms, or commitment to principle." Altruists tend to view themselves as one with all of humanity rather than acting only in their behalf.

On the basis of their research, the Oliners found these salient characteristics of altruistic people:

+ They believed all people have universal similarities.

+ The altruistic people they studied valued human relationships more than money or power.

+ Their commitment to caring extended far beyond their family and loved ones.

+ They felt a personal responsibility for helping relieve others' pain and sadness.

One of the threads that is woven throughout these rescuer's accounts and others demonstrating kindness is *empathy*. Empathy is the emotion that connects person to person. When one feels empathy for another in need or pain, it is hard to turn one's back on them. Conversely, as military propagandists know, turning a person into an "enemy" is to diminish or destroy the empathic connection. Lack of empathy makes it easier to kill them. For example, in the minds of WWII Americans, the German soldier becomes the "godless Kraut."

People demonstrating altruism are neither saints, extraordinary people or are they particularly religious in traditional terms. They simply have a very positive view of people in general, and are concerned about their welfare, and they take personal responsibility for how people are doing. The Oliners summed up the rescuers in their study as not saints, but ordinary people who nonetheless were capable of overcoming their human frailties by virtue of their caring capacities...They remind us that such courage is not in the providence of the independent and the intellectually superior thinkers but that it is available to all of us through the virtues of *connectedness, commitment and the quality of relationships developed in ordinary human interaction* (italics mine).

David E. Mullen, Ph.D.

THE CONSEQUENCES OF KINDNESS

The effects of kindness on both the recipient and givers have been discussed. It is tempting to think that kindness is a "one-way street," but kindness can go both ways. What have we learned?

One of the major effects of kindness is volunteerism. A recent Gallup Survey revealed that 52 percent of all American adults and 53 percent of all American teenagers are involved in some sort of volunteer work. When asked why, the common answer is "they want to help people." The instinct to help starts at an early age; as early as the second year of life, a child will respond to someone in distress by reaching out with a comforting touch, offering a favorite toy, or bringing a parent to help.

Some evidence suggests that volunteerism is associated with many measures of mental and physical help. For example, after studying three thousand volunteers, Drs. Allen Luks and Howard Andrews found twofold health benefits from volunteer work. They described the "healthy-helper syndrome." In the first stage, 95% of the volunteers experienced a "helper's high": increase of energy, sudden warmth and a sense of euphoria. These physical sensations, the researchers suggest, are due to the release of endorphins, natural mood elevators in the brain, in response to the act of helping.

The second stage, which more than half of the volunteers reported, is a longer-lasting sense of calm and heightened emotional well being. Luks and Andrews believe that the "helpers high" associated with volunteering is a powerful antidote to stress and a way to combat feelings of helplessness and depression. 5

Harvard cardiologist Herbert Benson believes that helping others works much the same way as yoga, spirituality, and meditation to help people "forget oneself, to experience decreased metabolic rates and blood pressure, heart rate, and other health benefits. Under stress, "...the heart pumps faster; the adrenal glands release corticosteroids (the 'stress hormones'), organ functions are disrupted; breathing speeds up. As a result the person is more sensitive to pain-and the 'stress hormones' that start coursing through the veins raise the level of blood cholesterol, elevate blood sugar, and reduce functioning of the immune system."[6]

Volunteering works the opposite way, reducing the effects of stress. It works so effectively that people in various studies have reported treating their stress-induced illness by engaging in volunteer work. Psychiatrist Milton Erickson once worked with a very severely depressed woman whose husband had died the previous year. She had become very withdrawn, isolating herself from friends and activities and found little satisfaction and pleasure in life. He learned that before her husband's death she had been very active in her church and enjoyed growing African violets. His therapy with her primarily consisted of having her get from the church each week a list of the shut-ins and those in the hospital. Her assignment was to deliver a violet plant to these persons. This was her therapy. After a while, her depression lifted. When the woman died, the church was overflowing with people who had come to pay their respects to the "African Violet Lady."

In addition to volunteerism, groups worldwide have emerged to promote kindness. About a decade ago, a "small kindness movement" started in Japan. A conference was held and its attendees spread the word to a number of nations. In America, the best-known kindness group is The Random Acts of Kindness Foundation. It acts as a "resource for people committed to spreading kindness." The Foundation's website offers materials, such as activity ideas, lesson plans, project plans, teachers' guides, publicity guides and workplace resources. The resources are free. The Foundation is privately funded, accepts no donations, grants and membership fees. Its purpose is to inspire people to practice kindness and "to pass it on" to others.

The practice of random acts of kindness was beautifully portrayed in the movie *Pay It Forward* a few years ago. The main character was Trevor, an eleven-year-old boy, who decided that his school project would be to randomly select three people to be the recipients of kindness. When they received it, they were instructed to pass it on. One of the themes of the movie was the ripple effect of kindness. Showing kindness without expecting anything in return often yielded unpredictable results. The other theme was that one caring person could make a difference in an often-uncaring world if he or she is attuned to people and situations where he can help.

HOW PARENTS CAN HELP THEIR CHILDREN TO BECOME KIND

What can parents do to help their children develop a sense of compassion and caring for others? It begins in the home. The American Psychological Association's Public Affairs Office offers some specific suggestions.

Parents need to let their children know how much it means to them they believe in kindness and responsibility.

"When you catch your child doing something that you think is thoughtless or cruel, you should let them know right away that you don't want them doing that. Speak to your child firmly and honestly, and keep your focus on the act, not on the child personally: something along the lines of "What you did is not very nice" rather that "You are not very nice!"

Parents need to be role models for their children. According to a study by psychologists E. Gil Clary, Ph.D., and Jude Miller, Ph.D., there are two kinds of parental role modeling that help teach children to be caring: kindness to others, and kindness to the child. If the parents are caring and compassionate, it's more likely their children will be too. Children watch their parents and other adults for clues on how to behave. Giving money and a kind word to a homeless person, taking a stray animal to a shelter, doing a favor for a neighbor, paying the toll for the person behind you are small acts of kindness that your children can observe. Encouraging your children to participate in a school drive to raise money for a family in need is an important way to get involved.

The parent's kindness to the child is extremely important. A child learns respect and kindness by how his parents treat him. If he is treated that he has value and worth, he can be helped to understand that all living creatures have worth and should be treated respectfully and with kindness.

While it is important to let your children know how strongly you feel about their unkind acts, it is also important to let them know how highly you regard their kind ones. For instance: "I saw you take care of the boy who fell on the playground. That was very kind of you, and it makes me feel very proud."

What most motivates a child to grow up caring about others is the caring the child receives. Experts point out that when children feel a more secure base at home, they are more likely to venture out and pay attention to others; it is when they feel deprived of love and nurturing that they focus on themselves and their own needs.

In conclusion, kindness is sometimes viewed as a virtue reserved for old maid aunts or grandmothers. However, each of us can practice acts of kindness. It is one of the most powerful forces in the world. No wonder when near the end of his life, Rabbi Abraham Joshua Heschel concluded: "When I was young, I used to admire intelligent people; as I grow older, I admire kind people."

EXERCISES

Dr. Sonja Lyubomirsky, professor of psychology at the University of California-Riverside, has tested whether asking people to "commit" five random acts of kindness would reliably increase their level of positive emotion. It does. [7] And it is most effective if all five acts are carried out on the same day.

Here are Sonja's instructions:

In our daily lives, we all perform acts of kindness for others. These acts may be large or small and the person for whom the act is performed may or may not be aware of the act. Examples include feeding a stranger's parking meter, donating blood, helping a friend with homework, visiting an elderly relative, or writing a thank you letter. One day each week, you are to perform five acts of kindness. The acts do not need to be for the same person, the person may or may not be aware of the act, and the act may or may not be similar to the acts listed above. Do not perform any acts that may place you or others in danger.

Here are some other suggestions for contributing to kindness in the world.

+ Pay for the person's order behind you in the drive-through line.

+ Leave a huge tip for a small check.

+ Compliment at least 2 people every day. Mean it.

+ The next time someone admires something of yours and you can afford to do without it, give it away.

+ Give someone else the gift of time. Do something for someone else that requires time and effort on your part.

10
INTEGRITY

So live that you wouldn't be ashamed to sell the family parrot to the town gossip.

Will Rogers

At the end of 2005, a year filled with natural disasters, an increasingly unpopular war, political wrangling, the word 7 million Americans turned to on the Merriam-Webster online website to understand it all was integrity. It topped the list of the diction aries 10 most frequently looked-up words. Comments Merriam-Webster president, John Morse: "I think the American people have isolated a very important issue for our society to be dealing with. The entire list gives us an interesting window that opens up into what people are thinking about in their lives."

Why is integrity important?

The purpose of this chapter is to present the case that without integrity it is highly unlikely that one can live what philosophers and some psychologists have described as the good and meaningful life. Moreover, without the practice of integrity in personal and public life, the political, economic and social structures are weakened.

INTEGRITY DEFINED

When we think of integrity, various words come to mind:

Walking the talk

Authentic, straightforward

What's on the inside is displayed on the outside

Open, honest and direct in dealing with others

Courage of one's convictions

Behavior matches one's values

Principled, honorable, fair, accountable, and responsible

One who has integrity is committed to moral and ethical standards even when making life's hard choices, choices, which may be clouded by stress, pressure to succeed, or temptation.

The word integrity comes from the Latin *integritas,* meaning wholeness. Many are perhaps more familiar with what integrity is not. Regrettably, on a too regular basis, the media has been full of stories of people who demonstrate little integrity in their dealing with others and how they damage others' wellbeing and livelihood. The scandals at Enron, World Com, and Tyco come to mind. High-powered individuals blinded by greed and arrogance use their positions to cause much pain for their employees and stockholders. Watergate, the Clinton-Lewinsky relationship, and the alleged lies about weapons of mass destruction in Iraq, the practice of some congressmen in high places using taxpayer money for their own pleasures are reminders of the Greek philosopher's plaintive cry, where do you find an honest man?

Integrity is important in relationships. From the individual to the community to the nation, it is a key ingredient of trust. Trust is the glue that makes community life possible. Trust says, "I can count on what you say you will do. I can depend upon you. I believe that you will act toward me with respect and fairness." For example, if cheating rather than honesty becomes the norm, than we are in big trouble. I read a study recently about the huge percentage of college students who say that cheating is okay and necessary to get good grades and, thus, a good job upon graduation. We must rely on the good faith of others every day. If not, we could not put money in the bank, buy food, clothing, or medicine from others, drive across a bridge, get on a plane, go to the doctor—the list is endless. There are many examples of the vast harm that is caused when individuals forget or ignore the effect their dishonesty can have.

The greatest fallout from a lack of integrity is the loss of trust in institutions, industries and individuals. In the vacuum created when trust is lost, suspicion and paranoia thrive. Is it any wonder that we have lost faith in our institutions, management, the business world and those who lead us, and have become distrusting and cynical about the ability of those in authority to give priority to our welfare and wellbeing?

Integrity is commonly thought of as acting from one's convictions, being single minded in honoring and expressing ethical and moral commitments. On this basis, one might debate whether infamous leaders such as Hitler, David Koresh, and Osama Bin Laden could be said to have integrity. They adhere to a set of values that are clear and well communicated. They also have a clear sense of purpose. However, what keeps this from being true integrity is their not treating others with care. Their beliefs led to death and destruction for those who opposed them and who were judged not to be in sync with their philosophies.

In my opinion, integrity has two characteristics: 1) a relationship to self that is defined by a growing degree of wholeness; and 2) a relationship to others characterized by sensitivity to human needs informed by one's ethics and morality.

RELATIONSHIP TO SELF

Integrity is about connection, finding that balance between inner and outer life, between one's values and behavior. William Shakespeare wrote, "To thine own self be true, and it must follow, as the night the day, thou canst not then be false to any man." Carl Jung, centuries later, said that the purpose of life is to become whole. In fact, he called the process of becoming authentic and real individuation, which is from the Latin *individuous* which means "whole."

A while back, there was a story about Reuben Gonzalez, who was in the final match of his first professional racquetball tournament. He was playing the perennial champion for his first shot at a win on the pro circuit. At match point in the fifth and final game, Gonzalez made a super kill shot into front corner to win the tournament. The referee called it good, and one of the lineman confirmed that Gonzalez was the winner.

But after a moment's hesitation, Gonzalez turned and declared that his shot had skipped into hitting the floor first. As a result, the serve went to his opponent, who went on to win the match.

Reuben Gonzalez walked off the court; everyone was stunned. The next issue of a leading racquetball magazine featured Gonzalez on its cover. The lead editorial searched and questioned for an explanation for the first ever occurrence of a winner disqualifying himself on the professional racquetball circuit. Who could ever imagine it in any endeavor? Here was a player with everything officially in his favor, with victory in his grasp, who disqualifies himself at match point and loses.

When asked why he did it, Gonzalez replied, "It was the only thing I could do to maintain my integrity." Gonzalez was being true to himself. He was demonstrating that wholeness (the outer matching the inner) that Jung talked about.

Rather than wholeness, disconnection seems to be the malady of many individuals today. We read of family members being disconnected from one another, couples being disconnected and individuals disconnected from themselves. In Arthur Miller's classic play on the American gospel of success, *Death of a Salesman,* at Willy Loman's funeral, it was said of him: "He didn't know who he was." Loman was not connected to himself. He was divided within.

A powerful image of the divided self comes from the Indian *Bhagadvita* where an individual in a chariot is pictured trying to control three horses that pull him in different directions. Without a center, an inner compass, the charioteer loses control and is destroyed. Without a core set of values, such a person becomes like the proverbial chameleon changing its color to adapt to the particular environment. My grandmother used to tell me, "He who does not stand for something will fall for anything." The end result is that we lose a sense of who we are. The worst decisions we make are not the ones that lead to failure but the ones that leave us disappointed in ourselves. These are the decisions that disconnect us from ourselves. Unless the connection to yourself is honored and tended to, success will not succeed."

Our core values influence and shape who we are. We learn perhaps what our core values are when we are in situations that challenge and test us. Iron becomes strong only when in its crude form the impurities are removed under high heat. An old saying goes, "The true test of a man is what he proves to be in an emergency." When the days are filled with sunshine and blue skies, we seldom learn very much about ourselves and what deep down we really believe. But when the heavy rains come with thunder and lightning, we are faced with what we are really about. In an emergency or crisis (i.e., loss of a job, illness, divorce, death of a loved one), we discover what kind of stuff we are made of. In other words, adversity does not create character so much as it reveals it.

In the early years of our country when the colonists fought the British for independence, Nathan Hale was captured by the British and sentenced to be hung. His stirring words many school age children can still recall: "I regret that I have but one life to give for my country." Loyalty to his country was part of his integrity. When noted Russian author Leo Tolstoy was on his deathbed, his final words were reported to have been, "…love, love…only love." This was one of his core beliefs, an essential ingredient of his integrity. When I was a teenager, I read *The Diary of Anne Frank*. These were writings of a young girl who with her family hid in an attic during WWII until their capture by the Gestapo.

The Frank's family life was later depicted in a powerful movie. Like many teenage girls, she kept a diary, recording her innermost thoughts and feelings. What makes reading the diary so poignant is knowing that her brief life was snuffed out in a Nazi gas chamber. In that unfinished diary near the end, Anne wrote, "In the end, I believe deep down that people are good." Despite the worst in human nature that she and her fellow Jews experienced at the hand of Hitler, she still held to a core belief in the value of others. Our integrity is revealed when we deal with adversity.

Harvard psychiatrist Dr. Edward Hallowell tells of a Harvard student who came to see him because he was depressed. This student wanted to be on the top and did not care how he got there. Hallowell tried to get him to look at the cost of such a pursuit. The student replied,

"I don't care. Just as long as I am the one who finishes first."

"But first at what?" Hallowell persisted.

"It doesn't matter!" The student yelled back at him.

"But it does matter," Hallowell replied, "If you become the best at something you don't believe in, it won't make you happy."

"Dr. Hallowell, I think you are naïve," he answered. "Do you think the man who invented Tupperware believes in Tupperware? Do you think the president of Cambridge Savings believes in what he is doing? Do you think the average senior partner at Hale and Don believes in his job? Of course not! They all believe in how many people they can order around! I mean, I hate to tell you this because you are basically in a loser's profession, but what really matters is sitting in the first row!"

Hallowell replied, "It must be hard to want to be on top so badly, and yet not have any guarantees."

"Yes, it is hard. But the solution is not to try to sell me on the cheap seats in life, which is what I think you are trying to do. I want the front row."

"Honestly, Jason," Hallowell replied, "I am not trying to sell you on the cheap seats. It's just that I know from experience that there are a lot of unhappy people in the front row, and a lot of happy people in the cheap seats."

"Like you?" Jason asked. "Are you happy in the cheap seats? Well, I'd rather be miserable in the front row than happy in the cheap seats. That's what I am."

"But you don't have to be that way," Hallowell continued. "After all, the reason you are coming to see me is that you are not happy in life doing things the way you have been doing them."

"Touché," Jason replied, with a slight grin. [1]

The point of this example is that our outer life must match our inner life or, like Jason, we will experience turmoil, restlessness and unhappiness. This is where integrity comes in. It is the inner compass that provides direction. It helps us to look to ourselves. When we are lost in the forest at night, we need a North Star to guide us.

The Italian industrialist France Bernable was appointed CEO of a company in 1992 that was debt ridden and government owned. He took the company and transformed it into a thriving company. In reflecting on what he did, he said in an interview published in *The Harvard Business Review* in 1998:

> You can rely on no one. In Italian, we call this condition *solitudine.* If you are in a difficult situation, as I was for a very long time, then it can be dangerous to listen too much to others or to depend on them. You have to watch every bit of the picture. And then you need an inner compass to indicate the way. In my case, that compass was my conscience…the right thing to do was to pull the company out of the swamp

of politics it was mired in. My compass told me where to go and what I needed to do to get there.

A person is emotionally healthy to the degree he can genuinely disclose himself to another. That is, he is being real with the other. When he is feeling anger, he expresses it in appropriate ways. When sad, he expresses it. Integrity includes a genuine presentation of the self to others. What you see is what you get. Studies have shown that self-disclosure has important physical as well as emotional benefits. Put another way, deceitfulness, posturing, and insincerity are not good for our well being. They are the opposites of integrity.

RELATIONSHIP TO OTHERS

Integrity also involves a sensitivity to human needs that is informed by one's ethics and morality. This is integrity with its sleeves rolled up. As mentioned earlier, despots and dictators like Stalin, Hitler, and

Idi Amin meet the first part of integrity's definition: being of one piece, commitment to a set of values that are clear and well-communicated. What is missing, of course, is *their treatment with others with care and respect.* Integrity looks both within and without.

Isn't this the reason why many admire the Dahli Llama, Mother Teresa or Nelson Mandela? They walk their talk. Upon his release from twenty-five years of imprisonment in an Apartheid South Africa, Mandela forgave his captors and invited them to participate in the new multi-racial government he was forming. Think of Mother Teresa taking seriously Christ's invitation to minister to the "least of these" (the lepers, terminally ill, and the homeless) in the slums of Calcutta. This remarkable woman once was asked what her life was about. She replied simply, "My life is caring for my beloved Christ in his most distressing disguises." What a powerful way of walking the talk.

While these individuals received the international spotlight for what they did, there are countless examples of ordinary people whose integrity and caring for others shine as brightly! Recall the non-Jewish neighbors in a small midwestern town who rallied to their Jewish neighbors' support when they were the victims of hate crimes. Vandals broke the windows where Menorahs were burning. The non-Jewish neighbors put Menorahs in their windows. Think of the college age students who spend their spring break, not frolicking and partying at Daytona or Fort Lauderdale but pounding nails and sawing wallboard for Habitat for Humanity or in cleanup along the Gulf Coast ravaged by Hurricane Katrina. Or think of Paul Rusebagina, the unassuming Rwandan hotel manager whose true story is told in the film *Hotel Rwanda*. When the Hutu militia began a savage massacre of the Tutsi people, he risked his own life to shelter more than 1,200 people.

Recently I read the heart-warming story of Charles Moore. Moore, a 59-year-old homeless man, was living in Michigan. He had lost his roofing job in Ohio and had moved back to Michigan but couldn't find work.

He was struggling to make a living by searching for returnable bottles. On one of his many searches, he came across 31 U. S. Savings Bonds in a trash bin. He turned them into a homeless shelter where a staff member tracked down the family of the man who had owned them. The bond owner's son gave Moore $100. The local media got hold of the story. Touched by this man's honesty, people around Michigan and other states started sending Moore gifts and money. Two businessmen donated $1,200, a shopping spree and a lead on a job. One man sends him eight trash bags full of returnable bottles. Three others gave combined $2,500.

At last count, Moore had received over $4,000. Such honesty by an individual who has so little stirs a deep chord in many.

INTEGRITY AND MORAL COURAGE

Integrity comes into play is when we are faced with a moral dilemma. While many of us are not faced with the kind of moral challenge Rusebagina, the Rwandan hotel manager experienced, circumstances in daily living arise that challenge our standards of morality. Your son tells you that your best friend's son is bullying kids at school. At a business luncheon, an associate tells a racist or sexist joke. You know that a co-worker is falsifying an expense account. Should you speak up?

If you are not sure, you are in good company. "Most of us don't know how we'll respond to a moral dilemma until we confront it," says Walter Sinnott-Armstrong, PhD, a professor of philosophy at Dartmouth College.

Studies have shown that it's far too easy not to rock the boat. In famous experiments carried out in the 1960s, social psychologist Stanley Milgram, Ph.D., showed just how willing people were to persist in doing something they knew was wrong. Each volunteer asked another participant a series of questions. Every time the person being queried responded incorrectly, the questioner was told to press a button that delivered an increasingly strong current. There was, in fact, no shock: The people answering the questions were actors. But the subjects did not know that, and more than 60 percent went on pressing the button even when those on the receiving end cried out in feigned pain and begged their inquisitors to stop." [2]

There are, of course, many reasons why people don't stand up to injustices and wrongs. Some of the most common: we are taught to obey authority; we may be confused about the issues; we do not like to be in the spotlight. We may realize that speaking out has consequences: possible loss of job, prestige, and friends. Nevertheless, standing up for convictions is a crucial duty in an open society. Most people want to do what is right.

How can we strengthen our moral fiber before a crisis of ethics is upon us? Rushworth Kidder, PHD, author of the book *Moral Courage: Ethics in Action* and director of the Institute of Global Ethics provides some guidance.

1. *Cultivate good role models.* Examples of moral courage are more than simply inspiring. They give people the example they can act on principle. Read biographies of people such as Martin Luther King, Nelson Mandela, Golda Meier, and John Addams.

2. *Learn from experience.* Knowing from past experience that you can stand up and make a difference prepares us for future situations. In the late fifties as a student at a church-related college in a Southern state, others and I pressed the administration and board of trustees to admit qualified black students. We thought the college's policy of admitting only black students from outside the United States was

hypocritical with its stated aim of being a Christian college. We were willing to take a stand. The action was not for us but for others. The administration listened but did not change its policy. In retrospect some 45 years later, I now see that that action provided a model for me for the future to stand up for other moral causes: the Vietnam War, before the Roe-Wade decision counseling women who wanted abortions and directing them to safe places instead of back alleys.

3. *Seek advice from people you trust.* When faced with an ethical problem, talk with someone you respect who is not involved: religious leader, a close friend, or a family member. Talking to other people clarifies your own position and helps you enlist the support of others so that you don't have to stand completely alone on your principles.

4. *Take the Mom Test.* Would you feel uncomfortable telling Mom that you didn't take a stand? If so, then your conscience may be telling you something.

SUGGESTED EXERCISES

1. Write your own eulogy, describing how you want to be remembered. Then write about what you will need to do in your life to be remembered the way you would like. Include what challenges or obstacles you will face in order to reach this goal and how you might overcome them.

2. Write a letter to someone in the news whose integrity has impressed you.

3. The following exercises were adapted from a list complied by psychologist Jonathan Haidt at the University of Virginia.

    a. Refrain from telling small, white lies to friends (including insincere compliments).

If you do tell one, admit it and apologize right away.

b. Monitor yourself and make a list of every time you tell a lie, even if it's just one. Try to make your daily list shorter every day.

c. At the end of each day, identify those instances in which you were attempting to impress others or appear to be someone you are not. Resolve not to do so.

11
CAN POSITIVE PSYCHOLOGY SHOW US THE WAY?

This book has been written to apply some principles of positive psychology to living the good life. My hope is that the reader has seen how the cultivation and practice of signature strengths, gratitude, an optimistic and hopeful attitude and a resilient spirit can be important ingredients in the mix for a good life. No doubt, some readers will recognize that the emphases of positive psychology are similar to what the major spiritual traditions have talked about for centuries. In this sense, positive psychology emphases are as old as the Talmud, the New Testament and the Koran.

What is new and fresh about this approach is that many of its themes have been put to the test in the laboratory and the consulting room. For example, researchers have demonstrated that optimists are more effective problem solvers than their pessimistic cousins. Grateful people are less materialistic and less prejudiced than ungrateful people. These are important findings.

Positive psychology is not primarily about feeling good but dolng good. It is not about putting on a happy face but living a life in such a way that one of the byproducts is enduring happiness. It is not about having more creature comforts and technological gadgets than the next person but realizing that we all are a part of the global family and the necessity of sharing.

In my view, many mistakenly believe that positive psychology is primarily about seeking happiness. They believe this movement is an updated version of positive thinking. In its cover magazine article on positive psychology, *TIME* miscast the happy face as the media mascot for it. The media has hyped positive psychology. Look at the articles in the *Wall Street Journal* and *Newsweek*. Positive psychology is much more than a focus on happiness. It is more than a "Don't worry, be happy" mantra. It is about the study of human strengths, close relationships, successful aging, and enhancing productivity in the workplace and in the classroom.

As mentioned in previous chapters, positive psychology has sought a balance. It seeks to redress the historic emphasis of much psychiatry and psychology on human deficit and pathology. The individual is more than a diagnostic label. He is more than a stimulus-response organism.

The individual is a thinking, feeling, valuing, and behaving person. He has specific strengths and gifts which when applied in daily living lead to contentment and the good life. Positive psychology provides the tools to identify these strengths and gifts. This is an emphasis that is needed in our schools and other institutions. The encouraging news is that some school systems have instituted programs to apply this knowledge.

That I am a passionate positive psychologist who believes that this growing body of knowledge is too important not to share should be obvious. However, I am not blind to some of its limitations.

Here then, are my criticisms; one major, the other minor. In its vision of the good life, positive psychology does not deal with the realities of suffering and the problem of evil. To be complete, a view of optimal human nature needs to grapple with why people suffer. I am not referring to the suffering humans inflict upon another as a result of ignorance, arrogance or selfishness but suffering that is random and unexplainable. What tools can a positive psychology provide a family coping with a child dying of leukemia? How does a positive psychologist counsel a couple that lost everything in a killer tornado? What light does a positive psychology shine on the emergence of an Adolph Hitler or Idi-Amin? These are important and tough questions.

Positive psychology makes a case that the meaningful life is the one worth living and brings us the most happiness in the long term. It then goes on to state that such a life is possible when we commit ourselves to something larger than ourselves. In my view, a positive psychology needs to address this issue: how evil is viewed and dealt with in a positive psychology context.

A minor criticism is that it does not give sufficient credit to the works of humanistic psychologists Abraham Maslow and Carl Rogers. In the 1950"s and "60"s they established humanistic psychology to focus on what gave meaning to life, looking at the very subjects positive psychologists now take as their own. In their effort to become "scientific" psychologists have distanced themselves from the legacy of those pioneers. This is similar to what psychology did in its infancy to gain respectability: break away from its philosophical moorings. Positive psychology needs to do a more effective job of appreciating and describing how it builds on and goes beyond humanistic psychologies.

In conclusion, I would like to quote these excerpts from Nelson Mandella's Inaugural Speech, 1994.

We ask ourselves, "Who am I to be brilliant, gorgeous, talented, and fabulous? Actually, who are you not to be? You are a child of God. You're playing small doesn't serve the world. There is nothing enlightened about shrinking so that other people won't feel insecure around you.

We were born to manifest the glory of God that is within us. It's not just in some of us; it is in everyone. And when we let our own light shine, we unconsciously give other people permission to do the same. As we are liberated from our own fear, our presence automatically liberates others.

ENDNOTES

INTRODUCTION

1. M.H. Czikzentimihaly, "Positive Psychology: An Introduction, *American Psychologist,* Jan. 2000, p. 7.

2. M. E. Seligman, "Positive Psychology: An Introduction," *American Psychologist,* Jan. 2000, p. 7.

3. *Ibid.*

CHAPTER I, HAPPINESS

1. R. Inglehart, *Positive Psychology*

2. D. Myers, "The Funds, Friends, and Faith of Happy People,"*American Psychologist,* Jan. 2000, p. 57.

3. Allan Carr, *Positive Psychology* New York: Brunner-Routledge, 2004, p. 250.

4. Harker and Keltner

5. D. Myers, *op. cit.,* p. 63.

6. D. Myers, *op. cit.,* p. 200.

7. M. Seligman, *Learned Optimism,* (New York: Basic Books, 1988). P. 55.

CHAPTER 2, FLOW AND SIGNATURE STRENGTHS

1. Nick Bayliss, "Teaching Positive Psychology," *Positive Psychology in Practice,* (Hoboken, New Jersey: John Wiley, 2004). P. 211.

2. Donald Clifton, *Now Discover Your Strengths,* (New York: Free Press, 2001), p. 9.

3. Donald Clifton, *op. cit.,* p. 6.

4. Donald Clifton, *op. cit.,* p. 72.

5. Alan Carr, *op. cit.,* p, 61.

6. Mihaly Csikzentmihalyi, *Flow,* (New York: Harper and Row, 1990), p. 62.

CHAPTER 3, OPTIMISM

1. Ann Ranard, "The World Through Rose-Colored glasses,"*Health,* August: 1989, p. 58.

2. Charles Carver, "Optimism and Health,"*Mind/ Body Health,* (Boston, Mass: Allyn and Bacon, 1996), p. 516.

3. Charles Carver, *ibid.*

4. Christopher Peterson, "Optimism and Health," *Mind/Body Health,* (Boston, Mass: Allyn and Bacon, 1996), p. 511.

4. David Burns, *Feeling Good: The New Mood Therapy,* (New York: Morrow, 1980).

CHAPTER 4, HOPE

1. C. R. Snyder, "Hope Theory: A Member of the Positive Psychology Family, *"Handbook of Positive Psychology,* (New York: Oxford, 2002, p. 258.

2. Snyder, *ibid.*

CHAPTER 5, GRATITUDE

1. Abraham Maslow, *Religion, Values and Peak Experiences,"*(New York: Penguin, 1964), p. 67.

2. Robert Emmons, "Gratitude," *Character Strengths and Virtues: A Handbook and Classification,* (New York: Oxford, 2004), p. 556.

3. George Vaillant, *The Wisdom of the Ego,* (Cambridge, MA: Harvard Press, 1993).

4. David SteindlRast, *Gratefulness: The Heart of Prayer,* (New York: Paulist Press, 1985).

CHAPTER 6, FORGIVENESS

1. Michael E. McCullough & Charlotte vanOyen Witvliet, "The Psychology of Forgiveness," *The Handbook of Positive Psychology,* (New York: Oxford, 2002), p. 447.

2. R.D. Enright. & Coyle, C. T. "Researching the process model of forgiveness within psychological interventions," In E. L. Worthington (Ed.), *Dimensions of Forgiveness: Psychological and theological perspectives.* (Philadelphia: Templeton Foundation Press, 1998), pp. 139-161.

CHAPTER 7, SPIRITUALITY

1. Kenneth Pargament, "Spirituality: Discovering and Conserving the Sacred," *Handbook of Positive Psychology,*(New York: Oxford, 2002), p. 646.

2. *Ibid,* p. 648.

3. Harold Kushner. *Who Needs God?* (New York: Summit Books, 1989), p. 206.

CHAPTER 8, RESILIENCE

1. Paul Pearsall, *The Beethoven Factor,* (New York: Summit Books, 2003), p. 3.

2. George Bonanno, "Loss, Trauma and Human Resilience: Have We Underestimated the Human Capacity to Thrive After Extremely Aversive Events", *American Psychologist,* Jan. 2004.

3. *Ibid.*

4. Paul Pearsall, *op. cit.,* p. 37.

5. Viktor Frankl, *Man's Search for Meaning,* (Boston: Beacon Press, 1962), p. 89.

CHAPTER 9, KINDNESS

1. Ben Dean, "Kindness and the Case for Altruism,"*Authentic Happiness Coaching Newsletter,* 2, 24.

2. N. Eisenberg, , P.A. Miller, . M.A. Schuller,, Fabes, "The role of sympathy and altruistic traits in helping: A reexamination," *Journal of Personality,* 57, 41-67.

3. Samuel Oliner and Pearl M. Oliner, *The Altruistic Personality,"*New York: Macmillan, 1988.

4. *Mind/Body/Health,* p. 408.

5. Allan Luks, *The Healing Power of Doing Good: the Health and Spiritual Benefits of Helping Others,* New York: Ballantine Books, 1991.

6. *Mind/Body/Health,* p. 410.

7. S. Lyubomirsky, C. Tkach, and K. M. Sheldon. "Pursuing sustained happiness through random acts of kindness and counting one's blessings: Tests of two six-week interventions." (2004) Unpublished data, Department of Psychology, University of California, Riverside.

FOR FURTHER READING

Buckingham, M., & Clifton, D.O, (2001). *Now Discover Your Strengths.* New York: Free Press.

Csikzentmihalyi, M. (1990). *Flow: The Psychology of optimal experience.* New York: Harper and Row.

Frisch, M. (2006). *Quality of life therapy: Applying a life satisfaction approach to positive psychology and cognitive therapy.* Hoboken, N.J.: Wiley.

Keyes, C. M. & J. Haidt (Eds.), (2003). *Flourishing: Positive psychology and the life well-lived.* Washington, D.C.: American Psychological Association.

Myers, D.G. (1993). *The Pursuit of happiness.* New York: Avon.

Peterson, C., & Bossio, L.M. (1991). *Health and optimism.* New York: Free Press.

Snyder, C.R. (Ed.,). (2000). *Handbook of hope: Theory, measures, and applications.* San Diego, CA: Academic.

Seligman, M.E. P., (1995). *The optimistic child.* Boston: Houghton Mifflin.